W9-CBT-798

Flann O'Brien

Twayne's English Authors Series

Kinley E. Roby, Editor
Northeastern University

TEAS 485

Flann O'Brien
Courtesy of the Irish Times.

Flann O'Brien

Sue Asbee

Queen Mary College, University of London

Twayne Publishers · Boston
A Division of G. K. Hall & Co.

Flann O'Brien
Sue Asbee

Copyright 1991 by G. K. Hall & Co.
All rights reserved.
Published by Twayne Publishers
A division of G. K. Hall & Co.
70 Lincoln Street
Boston, Massachusetts 02111

Copyediting supervised by Barbara Sutton.
Book production by Janet Z. Reynolds.
Book design by Barbara Anderson.
Typeset by Black Dot Graphics, Freeport, Illinois

First published 1991
10 9 8 7 6 5 4 3 2 1

Library of Congress Cataloging-in-Publication Data

Asbee, Sue.
    Flann O'Brien / Sue Asbee.
        p.   cm. — (Twayne's English authors series ; TEAS 485)
    Includes bibliographical references and index.
    ISBN 0-8057-7001-1
    1. O'Brien, Flann. 1911-1966—Criticism and interpretation.
    I. Title.   II. Series.
    PR6O29.N56Z514   1991
    828'.91209—dc20

90-23666

For Roni, with love

Contents

Preface

Brian O'Nolan was a professional writer who was able to turn his hand, with varying success, to many different forms. Throughout this study I have referred to him by the name "Flann O'Brien," the name that four of his five novels were published under. In Ireland during his lifetime he was best known to the public at large for his newspaper column, "Cruiskeen Lawn," which appeared regularly in the *Irish Times*. This column was written under the pen name Myles na gCopaleen. He wrote a number of plays in the 1940s and television scripts in the early 1960s, as well as short stories and occasional critical essays. But it is in the guise of novelist that his most important and lasting work was written, though his two most influential novels were not recognized as such at the time. *At Swim-Two-Birds* was published in 1939. It was reasonably widely and favorably reviewed, but it was not a commercial success until it was reprinted in 1960. *The Third Policeman* was offered to various publishers in 1940, but all turned it down and it was not until after his death that the book came out, in 1967.

If he had written no other fiction at all, these two novels would be sufficient to establish O'Brien's reputation as innovative and important in twentieth-century literature. His imagination veered toward the fantastic and anarchic. He can be seen to fit into a long tradition of fiction written in English, as well as being a precursor of more recent trends. *At Swim-Two-Birds* is such an unusual book that it seems almost a disservice to mention the eighteenth-century *Tristram Shandy,* but Sterne's work can best be described as an antinovel, and if we want to make O'Brien "fit," one way to think of his first book is in this tradition, which includes Joyce's *Ulysses* and Woolf's *Orlando.*

At Swim-Two-Birds certainly owes something to the modernist writers of the early twentieth century, particularly in the interweaving of myth and contemporary events, the lack of plot, and the insistence on what one might think of as the less promising, seedier sides of life. But it is equally important to recognize that one reason for this "imitation" was to make fun of modernism. The book expresses a certain amount of dissatisfaction with the generally held modernist belief that art could be a substitute for religion. Typically, O'Brien does not address this view in a ponderous or even direct way, but by including random extracts from all manner of

previously published writing, he sends up the idea of seeming fragments
held together in a secure aesthetic framework. Some of his references and
allusions come from "respectable" literary sources, but he also includes,
for example, road safety rules copied from the back of an exercise book. It
is unlikely that he would have thought of himself as a postmodernist
writer, but effectively that is what he was. Postmodernism is a
much-disputed and difficult term, one that has been used to describe
diametrically opposed kinds of writing—the "new realism" of the
novelists of the fifties, for example, as well as the anarchy of William
Burroughs. But if the term is used to describe fiction that is deliberately
random and discontinuous, then it is possible to say that O'Brien was one
of the first to write in this way.

The Third Policeman is a very different work, but it shares At Swim's
black humor and bleak vision of human isolation; like At Swim it is an
extraordinarily funny book. These things may sound like contradictions,
but O'Brien's talent lies in synthesizing such disparate elements. The
Third Policeman also demonstrates O'Brien's brilliant narrative technique;
he deceives his readers throughout, but when the book is reread, it has to
be admitted that no underhand tricks have been played. If it displays his
skill in handling narrative, it is also a tribute to the human imagination
—at its most bizarre and uncomfortable. William Golding achieved
something similar in Pincher Martin, a book written many years after The
Third Policeman but published 10 years before O'Brien's book appeared.

An Béal Bocht (The Poor Mouth) followed The Third Policeman, and is
different again. It was written in Irish, and published under O'Brien's
"Myles" pseudonym. Like all his fiction, it is a comic work, but the
darker side of comedy is never far from the surface. The Poor Mouth
depends partly on the vogue for Irish biography from remote areas of the
country. O'Brien himself was defensive of the Irish language—he was
brought up to be bilingual—but he had no patience with fanaticism,
and it is the fanatics rather than the honest accounts of rural life that he
parodies. The later novels, The Hard Life and The Dalkey Archive, are
interesting mainly because of the earlier works; it is unlikely that they
would remain in print were it not for later recognition of O'Brien's
considerable earlier achievement.

This particular study concentrates on the novels, using O'Brien's other
writing to support arguments, rather than providing a detailed examination of his journalism and abilities as a playwright. As a dramatist,
whether for the stage or television, he was not particularly talented; his
plays are workmanlike rather than inspired. His journalism, on the other

hand, was frequently inspired, but not consistently so. This situation may have been owing to pressures of work as well as ill health, issues raised in the biographical chapter of this book. Some of his preoccupations in "Cruiskeen Lawn" are considered in the last chapter, together with a discussion of the deceptively simple short story "John Duffy's Brother," which encapsulates many characteristics of O'Brien's longer fiction.

O'Brien's reputation is already secure. More of his writing is in print today than ever was during his lifetime. Numerous articles have been published in literary journals on various aspects of his work, and many dissertations and theses have been written by students; but at the moment there is only one full-length critical introduction to his work, written by Anne Clissmann.

My methods throughout have been based on the Brian O'Nolan papers held by Special Collections at Southern Illinois University. I have quoted from letters O'Brien wrote when he was engaged in writing his novels—there are none, unfortunately, for *At Swim-Two-Birds*—and taken these as a starting point. His postpublication letters are often interesting too. Although some of this material has been published before, the bulk of it has not, and it is owing to the generosity of Mrs. O'Nolan, O'Brien's widow, that extracts from his letters appear here.

Acknowledgments

My biggest debt and greatest thanks are due to Evelyn O'Nolan for allowing me to quote freely from her husband's papers and published work, and to Special Collections, Morris Library, Southern Illinois University, Carbondale, which holds the O'Nolan papers. I would also like to thank the following writers and publishers for granting copyright permission: the *Irish Times,* for the photograph that appears at the front of this book; the Lilliput Press, for quotations from John Ryan's *Remembering How We Stood;* Martin Brian & O'Keeffe Ltd., for quotations from *Myles, Portraits of Brian O'Nolan,* edited by Timothy O'Keeffe; and Oxford University Press, for quotations from Tomás Ó Crohan's *The Islandman.* Malcolm Bradbury, John Fowles, Alasdair Gray, and John Wyse Jackson were all kind enough to find time to answer my inquiries on various points, kindnesses for which I am most grateful. I apologize to anyone I have tried and failed to reach, and to anyone I may have overlooked.

I would also like to thank my son Roni and "that lot," Judith, Terence, and Tom, for welcome diversions while I was writing this book. Eternal thanks to Margaret Elizabeth Parr (née Asbee).

Chronology

1911   Brian O'Nolan born 5 October at The Bowling Green, Strabane, County Tyrone, the third child of Michael and Agnes (Gormley) O'Nolan.

1916   The Easter Rising. The O'Nolan family living in Inchicore, Dublin.

1917   The family moves back to Strabane.

1922   James Joyce's *Ulysses* published.

1923   The family moves to 25 Herbert Place, Dublin. Brian and his eldest brothers go to school for the first time, attending Synge Street School.

1927   The family moves to Avoca Terrace in Blackrock; the boys attend Blackrock College.

1929   Brian enters University College, Dublin, in October.

1932   Awarded B.A. with honors in German, English, and Irish.

1933   Awarded traveling scholarship for study in Germany. Brian abroad during winter, and spring of the following year.

1935   Awarded M.A. for his thesis on Irish nature poetry. Starts work for the civil service in the Department of Local Government.

1938   Samuel Beckett's *Murphy* published.

1939   *At Swim-Two-Birds.* James Joyce's *Finnegans Wake* published. Outbreak of World War II; Ireland in a state of emergency. *The Third Policeman* written, but not published.

1940   The first "Cruiskeen Lawn" column appears in the *Irish Times.*

1941   *An Béal Bocht (The Poor Mouth).* James Joyce dies.

1943   *Faustus Kelly, Thirst,* and *The Insect Play* performed.

1944   To New York in July and August.

1948   Marries Evelyn McDonnell on 2 December.

1953   Retires from the civil service, owing to ill health. Continues to write for the *Irish Times* and various provincial papers.

1960   *At Swim-Two-Birds* republished.

1961   *The Hard Life.* Starts writing televison scripts.

1964   *The Dalkey Archive.* Starts work on *Slattery's Sago Saga* (unfin-
       ished). Hugh Leonard's adaptation of *The Dalkey Archive, The
       Saints Go Cycling In,* performed at the Gate Theatre.

1966   Dies in hospital, 1 April.

1967   *The Third Policeman* published posthumously.

Chapter One

Brian O'Nolan–Flann O'Brien

"I take plenty of strong drink, use bad language, and know everybody"[1] —that is how Flann O'Brien described himself on one occasion when he was asked for biographical information. It is at least partly accurate, but it is also characteristic, for although he summed himself up in such unflattering terms, he gave away no personal details—the same could be said about a stranger observed for a couple of hours in a bar. In O'Brien's case, "everybody" referred to writers, publishers, newspaper editors— anyone of literary importance in Dublin from the 1930s until the mid-1960s. "I don't believe any author should put his own personal real name. His work should be apart from his actual personality,"[2] he said on another occasion. This belief was firmly held, and it discourages attempts to draw parallels between his life and work. Brian O'Nolan published nothing under his own "personal real name." Four novels were written under the pseudonym "Flann O'Brien"; a fifth, in Irish, came out by "Myles na gCopaleen"—the name under which he wrote his *Irish Times* column. Short stories and articles in other newspapers and journals came out under such names as John James Doe and George Knowall; as a student he wrote fantastic "autobiographical" accounts for the college magazine using the invented name and persona of "Brother Barnabas." But he was best known as Flann O'Brien and Myles na gCopaleen.

O'Brien was born in 1911, the third in a family of 12 children; but there is a certain amount of doubt about the precise date—the kind of misconception he loved to encourage: "Two certificates attest severally that I was born on October 5 and that on 28 July of the same year a sister had been born. A wise old doctor has said that one of several possibilities is to be admitted: either, or possibly both, of the certificates was faulty—registration in the old days being left to illiterate midwives; one of the children was a mis-registered bastard, or the mother was a monster who had fabulous breed."[3] Brian's parents married in 1906 and their first three children were boys. It is likely, then, that his sister's birth certificate was incorrectly dated, but it is typical of Brian O'Nolan to develop a discrepancy such as this one into a flight of fancy.

He cultivated and encouraged myths, partly from a love of the fantastic, partly to protect his private life. In 1943 he told an interviewer from *Time* magazine that he had married Clara Ungerland, the daughter of a German basket weaver, when he was 32. She was blond and played the violin—but died a month after their marriage. The whole episode was complete invention, and O'Brien later said that it was a "superb heap of twaddle that would deceive nobody of 10 years of age."[4] But it was published in good faith, and such myths tend to be perpetuated—so much so that Nigel Andrew, reviewing an illustrated biography in the *Listener* in 1988, asks, "What was he up to in Germany in the 1930s? Did he, as he claimed, get married there?" The answer to the first question is that O'Brien claimed that he won a scholarship to Cologne University (though the institution holds no records of his presence); the answer to the second is no, he did not marry until 1948—and did so then in Dublin. O'Brien would have been delighted at the endurance of the apocryphal story.

He left no real autobiographical accounts. A younger brother, Kevin, wrote a short biographical essay for a volume of memoirs by friends and contemporaries of O'Brien's, and Ciarán O'Nolan, his brother, wrote an account, in Irish, called *Óige An Dearthár (The Brothers' Youth)*. Kevin describes his childhood and says that "the whole family had the same upbringing, more or less, and a certain community of experience."[5] The children spoke Irish among themselves. Their father, Michael Victor O'Nolan, was involved with the Gaelic League and spoke and taught Irish. He married Agnes Gormley who spoke English, and so the children grew up to be fluent in both languages.

Michael O'Nolan worked as a civil servant with the Customs and Excise Department, a job that required a certain amount of moving about the country. Brian was born in Strabane, County Tyrone, and with the rest of his brothers and sisters he was educated by his parents. For a short time a young woman, Miss Boyle, gave them lessons at home; she was succeeded briefly by a Mr. Collins, but eventually their father decided to embark on correspondence courses during his absences from home. These courses took the form of letters from him to the three eldest boys, Gearóid, Ciarán, and Brian. Whatever their individual exercises consisted of, the lessons did not last for long. The boys were fortunate in that their father had a fairly extensive collection of books. Ciarán recalls that they read William Hazlitt, John Dryden, Daniel Defoe, Jane Austen, Robert Louis Stevenson, the Brontë sisters, Anthony Trollope, Edgar

Allan Poe, Arnold Bennett, H. G. Wells, James Stephens, and many others.

It was not until the family moved to Dublin in 1923 that the eldest children were sent to school. The three eldest, Gearóid, Ciarán, and Brian, went to the Christian Brothers' Synge Street School. Ciarán wryly recalls that his father "did not ask us if we wanted to go, or if it was against our principles."[6] The discipline of school after the freedom of their childhood up to this point must have been hard to bear; Ciarán says it was like "throwing a person into a fire, or dipping him into icy water."[7] They found themselves backward in mathematical subjects but in English and Irish, unsurprisingly given their wide reading, they were advanced— "mature and developed in their critical judgment."[8]

In 1927 the family moved to Blackrock, and five of the children, including Brian, went to Blackrock College, where they won prizes and established reputations as studious pupils. Kevin claims that this reputation was undeserved, and that they certainly had no time for doing homework. In later years, he, like Brian, doubted the value of the formal education of his day: "What we did at home, apart from reading anything in sight, was to take things apart to see how they worked—with the result that they often ceased to work—to dismantle clocks, to unscrew anything that could be unscrewed . . . all this may have been more destructive than writing exercises but educationally it was not inferior."[9]

It was at Blackrock College that Brian told the senior mathematics teacher that rugby players should be "taken behind the stand at Lansdowne Road and shot."[10] This remark is unlikely to have been a popular one—the college was well known for rugby and Lansdowne Road is a famous Irish ground. Physical prowess was not one of Brian's characteristics. He described himself as having "pyrosis, acute hammer toe, and a tendency towards piano leg."[11] Anthony Cronin remembered him as a "small man whose appearance combined elements of the priest, the baby-faced Chicago gangster, the petty-bourgeois malt drinker and the Dublin literary gent."[12]

The metamorphosis into "literary gent" began at University College, Dublin. According to his brother Ciarán, Brian had not shown any particular interest in writing up to that time. He left Blackrock College and entered the university in October 1929. Looking back, Niall Sheridan, a fellow student, says, "It seems to me that he burst on the scene fully equipped as a writer."[13] Certainly it was while O'Brien was at University College that he began writing his first novel, *At Swim Two-*

Birds (1939). O'Brien was part of a circle of friends and associates there who had literary as well as drinking interests in common. Cyril Cusack and Liam Redmond were contemporaries—both later became famous for their work in theater and cinema. Denis Devlin went on to become Irish ambassador to Italy. Donagh MacDonagh had a ready-made reputation: he was the son of Thomas MacDonagh, poet and commander general of Ireland's first Republican army, executed in the Easter Rising of 1916. Niall Sheridan, Denis Devlin, and Donagh MacDonagh all published poetry at one time or another. In later life MacDonagh edited *The Oxford Book of Irish Verse,* including in it two poems by Devlin and two poems—translations from the Irish—by Brian O'Nolan. Sheridan's translation from Catullus, "Ad Lesbiam," is also included. It dates from his time at University College and is proof of his own assertion that he was the original of Brinsley in *At Swim-Two-Birds.* When Kelly, Brinsley, and the narrator of the novel are drinking in Grogan's bar, Brinsley is moved to hold forth: "Ah Lesbia, said Brinsley. The finest thing I ever wrote. How many kisses, Lesbia, you ask, would serve to sate this hungry love of mine?" (38). The twelve lines of poetry in the novel are identical to the poem that appears in MacDonagh's collection, though they are printed as prose in *At Swim,* and punctuated by Kelly calling for three more glasses of stout.

MacDonagh published several volumes of his own poetry. His last, *A Warning to Conquerors* (1968), came out after his death, with an introduction written by Niall Sheridan. In 1934 he and Sheridan made their first publishing venture together, with a slender volume of poetry called *Twenty Poems.*

MacDonagh and Niall Montgomery—another University College associate and long-term friend—contributed to the first James Joyce Symposium, held in Dublin in 1967. O'Brien himself wrote an elliptic essay, "A Bash in the Tunnel," for a special James Joyce edition of the journal *Envoy,* which his friend John Ryan edited.[14]

The college magazine, *Comhthrom Féinne (Fair Play)* provided O'Brien's first forum for publishing humorous articles. By 1933 he was its editor. His contributions sometimes appeared under the Irish form of his name, Brian Ua Nualláin, but he also invented extravagant personas. Many ideas that he used later first saw the light of day in these pages. The Myles na gCopaleen Escort Service of the *Irish Times's* "Cruiskeen Lawn" had its conception in the article "Are You Lonely in the Restaurant?" The editor of *Comhthrom Féinne* identified this mental state as pernicious and morbid, and undertook to alleviate it—for a fee: *"Comhthrom Féinne* will provide

EATERS, varying in quality and price to suit every client. YOU NEED NO LONGER EAT ALONE. Hire one of our skilled Conversationalists, play and talk as you eat and avoid the farce of pretending you are a THINKER to whom his own kind is sufficient for the day." Rules, classes, and conditions of EATERS were carefully set out. There was, for example, "an excellent line of SPINELESS DUMMIES" who would listen to absolutely anything without protest: "these highly-skilled Eaters will nod (plain) and nod (with conviction, 1d extra each) at every point emphasised by the client."[15]

O'Brien also wrote as "Brother Barnabas," who soon became a figure of legendary proportions—"statesman, diplomat, international financier"—who appeared regularly in the magazine. He was born in 1691 and, according to his "official biography," became president of Ireland in 1945! In 1934 a "probably posthumous" account by Brother Barnabas appeared, entitled "Scenes in a Novel": "I am penning these lines, dear reader, under conditions of great emotional stress, being engaged, as I am, in the composition of a posthumous article." Renting Trotsky's villa in Paris, he complains about the lease and the drains. Such fantasy is endemic to the persona O'Brien created. It is an early use of an idea he later developed in *At Swim* of a fictional character refusing to do as his author requires. Brother Barnabas is writing a novel in which his character Carruthers MacDaid is required to rob a poor box in a church: "But no! Plot or no plot, it was not to be. 'Sorry old chap,' he said, 'but I absolutely can't do it.' . . . Knowing that he was a dyed-in-the-wool atheist, I had sent him to a revivalist prayer-meeting, purely for the purpose of scoffing and showing the reader the blackness of his soul. It appears that he remained to pray."[16] In *At Swim* the narrator claims that in a "satisfactory" novel it would be "undemocratic to compel characters to be uniformly good or bad or rich or poor. Each should be allowed a private life, self-determination and a decent standard of living" (25). Trellis, the novelist within the narrator's novel in *At Swim,* suffers physical torture at the hands of his rebellious fictional characters. Like Brother Barnabas's character MacDaid, one of Trellis's characters resolutely rejects his allotted role as villain and insists on leading a virtuous life.

O'Brien's fertile imagination generated many literary plans. Sheridan recalls that he and O'Brien were "constantly preoccupied with literary theories and with more mundane schemes to raise ready cash, a very scarce commodity in those days."[17] Brinsley in *At Swim-Two-Birds* has similar preoccupations: "There are two ways to make big money . . . to write a book or to make a book" (24). In his memoir Sheridan outlines some of their plans, which include applying the principles of the industrial revolution to literature, and also the writing of the "All-Purpose Opening Speech," which was to consist of "one endless sentence, grammatically correct, and so devoid of meaning that it could be used on any conceivable occasion."[18] O'Brien, delighted with the notion, decided it must be translated into "every known language": "If nation could speak fluently to nation, without any risk of communicating anything, international tension would decline. The Speech would be a major contribution to civilization." The "logic" expressed here is akin to that in O'Brien's novel *The Dalkey Archive* (1964) in which Mick proposes to render the mad scientist De Selby harmless by introducing him to James Joyce. Mick plans to persuade them both to devote their "not inconsiderable brains in consultation to some recondite, involuted and incomprehensible literary project, ending in publication of a book which would be commonly ignored and thus be no menace to universal sanity" (118).

The notion of the all-purpose speech belonged to O'Brien's student years, the Joyce/De Selby collaboration to much later life—clearly the paradoxical idea of language as a means of *non*communication was one he retained. The idea of the speech is entirely flippant, but it is worth remembering that as a joke it belongs to the years preceding 1939, when internationally there was a great deal of tension. Fluency and noncommunication would (if we pretend to take them seriously for a moment) give an illusion of concord and understanding, creating a veneer masking unresolved chaos and dissension.

Sheridan also gives an account of O'Brien's projected plan for the corporately produced "Great Irish Novel." O'Brien suggested that he, Devlin, MacDonagh, and Sheridan should jointly produce a work of fiction to be called *Children of Destiny*. His reasons for "making" a book (not, on this occasion, in the sense of setting up as a bookmaker) are worth considering: "A vast market was ready and waiting. Compulsory education had produced millions of semi-literates, who were partial to 'a good read.' So it must be a big book, weighing at least two-and-a-half pounds. We must give them length without depth, splendour without style. Existing works would be plundered wholesale for material, and the ingredients of the saga would be mainly violence, patriotism, sex, religion, politics and the pursuit of money and power. *Children of Destiny* would be the precursor of a new literary movement, the first masterpiece of the Ready-Made or Reach-Me-Down School."[19] *Children of Destiny* came to nothing, but it was about this time that O'Brien started work on *At Swim*. Sheridan implicitly invites readers to draw comparisons between O'Brien's projected literary interests and his narrator's interests in his first novel.

The idea of plundering existing works was one O'Brien takes to extremes in *At Swim-Two-Birds*—though oddly enough the result is a strikingly original novel. The "Ready-Made" movement is a typical example of the way in which O'Brien and his characters take ideas to their furthest logical conclusion: Sheridan does the same thing when he says that *Children of Destiny* must be big, "weighing at least two-and-a-half pounds." O'Brien certainly used "found" material in *At Swim*. Sheridan recalls showing him a letter from a tipster in Newmarket—a town in Suffolk famous for horse racing—and discovering later that it had been transcribed word for word in the next batch of manuscript O'Brien showed him.[20]

Sheridan's reminiscences establish a context for *At Swim*, indicating that many of the novel's preoccupations had counterparts in the literary interests of that group of talented students, O'Brien's contemporaries at University College. It seems extraordinary for a novel that is recognized as being highly experimental and avant-garde to have such a firm basis in personal relationships of the author's. On the other hand, what better way to introduce randomness into fiction than by allowing real life to be incorporated into it? Sheridan performed much the same role in real life as Brinsley does in the book—critic and audience to his friend's production: "I found myself (under the name of Brinsley) living a sort of double life at the autobiographical core of a work which was in the process of production."[21]

In 1932 O'Brien received a B.A. with second-class honors in German, English, and Irish. A travel scholarship he won in 1933 allowed him to study at the University of Cologne in Germany for about six months, and when he returned to Dublin he began working for an M.A. degree on the subject of Irish nature poetry.

O'Brien had little respect for formal education. During his childhood, intellectual stimulus came from other members of his family; at college his creative talents were fired mainly by association with fellow students. Looking back over his career at University College, he wrote in "Cruiskeen Lawn," not long before he died in 1966: "What have I to show for five years of my life? . . . I paid no attention whatsoever to books or study, and regarded lectures as a joke—which, in fact, they were if you discern anything funny in mawkish, obtuse mumblings on subjects any intelligent person could master in a few months. The exams I found childish and in fact the whole university concept I found to be a sham. . . . I sincerely believe that if university education were universally available and availed of, the country would collapse in one generation."[22] The Myles na gCopaleen persona is notoriously both extravagant and unreliable, but beneath the bombast there is a sense that O'Brien felt strongly about the subjects he returned to. His distrust of formal education generally and the examination system in particular is evident in this passage too: "Perhaps the English Honours Paper best illustrates what I am trying to say. . . . It is not so much that the student is expected to be familiar with the works of very many inferior persons, for after all what is literature but just this? What is disquieting and cannot be borne is that one is expected to admire or decry these things and that one will obtain marks and consequently be considered educated only in so far as one's admiration and contempt corresponds with those of the person who sets the paper."[23] This topic was one to which O'Brien returned again and again over the years.

He was also scathing of his tutor's, Douglas Hyde's, abilities. Hyde was later to become the first president of Ireland, but he was professor of Irish when O'Brien was at University College. O'Brien held him in high regard as a man with "a heart of gold" but maintained that Hyde spoke Irish "inaccurately and badly." "After some experience of his lectures," O'Brien wrote, "I decided to abstain from his tuition."[24]

Though he must have made some effort to obtain his degree, O'Brien claims to have spent most of his time playing billiards and poker. Other extracurricular activities at which he excelled were his involvement with *Comhthrom Féinne* and the Literary and Historical Society, a forum for wit and oratory. O'Brien won the gold medal for impromptu debate in 1933, a particular accolade as at that time he was unofficial leader of the opposition, not auditor of the society. He wrote his own recollection of the society for its centenary celebrations in 1955. Its audiences, he remembered, consisted of a

most heterogenous congregation, reeling about, shouting and singing in the hogarthian pallor of a single gas-jet (when somebody had not thought fit to extinguish the same) . . . and I had the honour to be acknowledged its president. It is worth noting that it contained people who were not students at all. A visitor would probably conclude that it was merely a gang of rowdies, dedicated to making a deafening uproar the *obbligato* to some unfortunate member's attempts to make a speech within. It was certainly a disorderly gang but its disorders were not aimless and stupid. It could nearly be claimed that the mob was merely a severe judge of the speakers.[25]

"The mob," however, quite clearly recognized and respected O'Brien's skills, whatever his subject matter might be.

Blather saw the light of day in 1934. It was a monthly magazine of which there were only five editions, and it was largely O'Brien's work. Like *Comhthrom Féinne* it has a lot in common with the later "Cruiskeen Lawn." *Blather* was introduced, ludicrously, as "the only paper exclusively devoted to the interests of clay-pigeon shooting in Ireland":

As we advance to make our bow, you will look in vain for signs of servility or for any evidence of a slavish desire to please. We are an arrogant and a depraved body of men. We are as proud as bantams and as vain as peacocks. *Blather doesn't care. . . . Blather* has no principles, no honour, no shame. Our objects are the fostering of graft and corruption in public life, the furtherance of cant and hypocrisy, the encouragement of humbug and hysteria, the glorification of greed and gombeenism. . . . Write to us for the address of your nearest *Blather* Study Circle. Write to us for a free cut-out pattern of the *Blather* Patent Woollen Panties and say good-bye to colds. Write to us for our pamphlet, "The *Blather* Attitude on Ping-Pong."[26]

In spite of all this activity, O'Brien was awarded his M.A. and left the university to join the civil service. He worked a five-and-a-half-day week in the Department of Local Government but completed *At Swim* over the next years anyway, finishing it in 1938. His career with the civil service lasted until he retired in 1953 — under something of a cloud, and at least partly to do with his drinking habits — but by this time he had worked his way up to being the principal officer for town planning and was awarded a pension.

He worked in the Department of Local Government under the supervision, at first, of John Garvin. They remained friends, and it was Garvin who supplied the Greek epigraph to *At Swim-Two-Birds*. He recalls that O'Brien kept up a "constant and delightful" correspondence with him when they moved to different departments. O'Brien sent him letters "from illiterates, nitwits and 'quare fellows' with appropriate comments. When I was dealing with the supervision of home assistance and administration he wrote enquiring whether I would regard the figures on the Parthenon frieze as coming within the statuory definition of outdoor relief."[27] This sense of the ridiculous helped O'Brien to retain his sanity in a job where he had nothing but contempt for his bourgeois assistants or for the "civil service overlords with striped trousers in the corridors of power whom he stigmatized as 'Kerry peasants in Treasury pants.' "[28]

While he was working for the civil service O'Brien made several trips abroad, traveling to England and the Continent for the purpose of gathering information and statistics. He made trips to the United States in 1944 and 1949—presumably making and renewing contact with American publishers while he was there.

At Swim-Two-Birds was published in 1939, a couple of months before the outbreak of World War II. Whether or not this international and continuing disaster had any real effect on the sales of the book, O'Brien chose to take it personally: "Adolf Hitler took serious exception to [the book] and in fact loathed it so much that he started World War II in order to torpedo it. In a grim irony that is not without charm, the book survived the war while Hitler did not."[29] *At Swim* was well reviewed and enjoyed an appreciative coterie audience in Dublin, but it was far from being a commercial success. It did not sell well generally until it was reissued as a Penguin Modern Classic in 1960.

O'Brien completed his second novel, *The Third Policeman,* in 1940, but his publishers declined it, saying that in their opinion he should be less fantastic than he had been in his first book, whereas he had become more so. O'Brien invented several stories in which he claimed that the *Third Policeman* manuscript was lost—probably in order to save face and hide his disappointment. In fact it was carefully preserved. *The Dalkey Archive* (1964) reworks some ideas from *The Third Policeman,* but there are also passages in the later novel that have quite clearly been transcribed directly from the rejected manuscript. There is no mystery attaching to it at all.

Literary activity of a spare-time or recreational nature continued to be important to O'Brien. His circle of literary-minded friends widened rather than diminished in spite of full-time civil service work. In *Remembering How We Stood* John Ryan recalls bohemian life in Dublin during the 1940s and 1950s. Sean O'Sullivan (the painter), J. P. Donleavy, Brendan Behan, Patrick Kavanagh, Anthony Cronin, and Flann O'Brien were among Ryan's friends and drinking companions. Inevitably Ryan places quite a lot of emphasis on the drinking fraternity: "Most Dubliners I knew then had an alcohol problem—*they couldn't get enough of it.*"[30] They patronized McDaid's, Byrnes, the Dolphin, the Bailey, the Pearl, and the Palace, as well as numerous other bars: "It was in the streets and pubs of Dublin that I met them in the middle nineteen-forties. Streets which echoed to the ring of hooves and wheels of steel, where along the noiseless wooden sets of Grafton Street brigades of cyclists would at tea-time invade the thoroughfare, while distantly the tram bells clanged."[31]

A state of national emergency had been declared in Ireland during World War II; petrol was severely rationed—partly accounting for the "ring of hooves and wheels of steel" rather than the noise of car exhausts in Ryan's description. Coal, natural gas, clothes, and shoes were rationed too, and sweets and cigarettes were scarce. But whiskey, according to Ryan, continued to pour "niagarously" in the Pearl and Palace bars.

Although the Irish Free State had been established in 1922, the new republic's policies were isolationist and the censorship-of-literature act that was passed had a deleterious effect on thought and progressive ideas. Ryan likens Ireland during the war to a "stifling greenhouse, more hermetically sealed than ever."[32] It is the poets and painters that he credits with Ireland's survival, not its priests or politicians. The writers and artists were "the keepers of the nation's conscience, those who injected sanity through humour—while partly losing their own in the process."[33]

It is in the character of keeper of the nation's conscience that O'Brien wrote many of his *Irish Times* columns—under his "Myles" designation. In one instance, and it was a subject he returned to, he roundly condemned the Dublin Corporation's refusal of Rouault's painting *Christ Crowned with Thorns*. The painting had been purchased by the Friends of the National Collections for £400 and was offered as a gift to the Municipal Gallery. The board of the gallery rejected the picture, variously describing it as "a travesty," "offensive to Christian sentiment," and "childishly naive and unintelligible." The painting was executed in a modern manner; Rouault himself, according to Myles, preserved silence on the controversy, refusing to be drawn into explanation or defense of his work. Whether O'Brien liked it himself he did not say, but in his opinion it could not be expected "to please persons whose knowledge of sacred art is derived from shiny chromo-lithograph bon-dieuiserie . . . examples of which are to be found in every decent Irishman's bedroom. Such persons, however, never enter picture galleries, and there is no reason why their opinions should be considered at all."[34]

This view is realistic rather than dismissive. O'Brien goes on to say that what is important is the attitude of the "intelligent" person, and then describes modern art in terms that are equally applicable to fiction—his own *At Swim-Two-Birds* in particular:

Many forms of art are devoid of rules. The artist makes his own. However formless or chaotic the manifestation, it is art if it expresses something, possibly something bad or negative. Even our own pathetic and untidy advance guards who have never learnt to draw are artists because they express artistically (and convincingly) the fact that they can't draw. But inasmuch as the modern artist makes his own rules, the onlooker must also be permitted to fix his own standards of appraisal. . . . The attitude of each individual to the picture is personal, and is not necessarily related to any conventional criteria.[35]

Strikingly, the passage contains none of Myles's usual irony. The onlooker must be able to fix his or her own standards, but as Myles goes on to say, that person must also take care to ensure that he or she is sufficiently well informed to make a judgment.

The association with the *Irish Times* began when O'Brien and Niall Sheridan, using pseudonyms, joined in a controversy being aired on the "letters" page—significantly enough on the subject of drama, Chekov's *The Three Sisters,* which was not playing to full houses in Dublin at the time. When the stir eventually died down, O'Brien and Sheridan started various bogus exchanges of their own, often holding opposing points of view on facetious topics under different names. A number of these exchanges have recently been collected and published, and the editor acknowledges the impossibility of establishing the true identity of "Lir O'Connor," "F. O'Brien," "Oscar Love," "Whit Cassidy," and others.[36] The style and humor are indistinguishable. "F. O'Brien" claims in his youth to have known Ibsen and to have listened to teatime discussions between him, Joseph Conrad, Swinburne, and George Moore. Ibsen, he observed, suffered from dandruff. Lir O'Connor wrote to object, claiming the allegation could not be true, as Ibsen wore a wig. He offered as evidence his recollection of Ibsen's wig falling into a soup tureen. Irrelevant and irreverent, such fabrications and absurdities were popular and boosted the newspaper's circulation considerably. Eventually R. M. Smyllie, the editor, asked Sheridan to introduce him to O'Brien and suggested that he write a regular column for the paper. The first contributions were written in Irish, then some appeared in English. Eventually English became the usual medium, always under the Irish title "Cruiskeen Lawn," which means "Full Little Jug."

The column was a success, but writing to deadlines day after day, as well as working full-time, must have been a great strain. Anthony Cronin says that though O'Brien was proud of his newspaper work, the "terrible burden" was probably as ruinous in the long run as the drink was: "He would often rehearse a joke that was to appear a few days later and he was always pleased if you adverted to something that had been in it, but it must have torn his guts out over the years. The fact that it was humorous in intent and that he could and did adopt any one of a multitude of ironic levels saved him to some extent from becoming the cantankerous preacher, the corrector and arranger, but it was a temptation to him nonetheless, particularly in the later, more embittered years."[37]

By 1960, when he had retired from the civil service, O'Brien referred to his work for the *Irish Times* as "slavery": "I am most anxious to leave the dirty *Irish Times*. It was an odd enough paper in Smyllie's day but it has now become really quite intolerable. I need not discourse to you on their shocking notions of pay but in addition much of the material I send in is suppressed and for that work they pay nothing whatever. Other articles are mutilated and cut, often through sheer ignorance. . . . Generally, the whole outfit is insufferable."[38]

O'Brien's description of himself as one who takes "plenty of strong drink" and uses bad language might well have had something to do with his early retirement, and probably just as much with his dissatisfaction with the *Irish Times*. In Cronin's opinion, O'Brien was a "true alcoholic" —much more so than Brendan Behan, whose excesses were notorious and noisier. O'Brien had "an inbuilt psychological need for alcohol. . . . He was a sober drinker, meticulous and methodical. He seldom drank anything but Irish whiskey. . . . He was inclined to be cantankerous, but had no interest in fun and games. Drink and the monologue which was his idea of conversation sufficed him."[39]

O'Brien cannot have been an easy man to live with. He married in 1948, but the couple had no children and his wife, Evelyn, seems to have made little or no impact on the hardworking, hard-drinking routine that made up his life. His wife, like the rest of his family, was not a part of his public side. By all accounts his family affections ran deep, and they were, if not sacrosanct, then not to be discussed lightly, if at all. Friends could be transformed into fictional characters in his books; family members were not.

In spite of the company he kept, O'Brien was "the reverse of bohemian." He was a quiet man to whom the thought of sexual promiscuity was abhorrent,[40] but he was not particularly prudish about such behavior in others. Brendan Behan, for example, led a much more colorful life than he did, and O'Brien was not blind "to the fact that [Behan's] a lout and sometimes something worse"[41] but still considered Behan to be a friend.

In 1954, realizing that this year marked the fiftieth anniversary of the events of *Ulysses,* O'Brien and John Ryan decided to organize their own "Bloomsday" celebrations. Various carefully selected friends were invited to join them on their "prilgrimace"—a contraction of *pilgrimage, grimace,* and *disgrace.*[42] It was to take place, as *Ulysses* does, on 16 June and to start at the Martello Tower, where the book begins, and follow its movement to Dalkey, where Stephen goes to receive his pay, then on to Sandymount Strand and back into Dublin itself for the opening of the fourth chapter with Bloom on Eccles Street, and so on. Drinking in the Ormond Hotel, Barney Kiernan's, Davy Byrnes's, and the Bailey at the appropriate times of the day dictated by Joyce's work would inevitably form an important part of the celebrations.

O'Brien and Ryan agreed that Con Levanthal should symbolize Bloom—though he should be kept in ignorance of the fact—because of reasons pertaining to his being Jewish. Anthony Cronin, in those days a youthful poet, should represent Stephen Dedalus. O'Brien himself should stand for Simon Dedalus and Martin Cunningham, while John Ryan, because he was an editor, should be Miles Crawford. Patrick Kavanagh was the Muse, and Tom Joyce represented the family: he was a cousin of James Joyce's, a dentist who had never read *Ulysses.*

The Bloomsday celebration started, as planned, from the Martello Tower, but as Ryan recalls: "More pubs were visited *en route* than even the most faithful adherence to the Joyce master-plan demanded. By the time we reached the purlieus of Duke Street ('Lestrygonians'), communications became unreliable, transport broke down, and the strict order of procedure was allowed to lapse."[43] The celebrants had hired two elderly horse cabs for the occasion—of the kind that were commonly used in 1904, some of which were still about on the streets of Dublin in 1954. John Ryan and Anthony Cronin both remember the day equally vividly, but slightly differently; however, photographs and even a color movie testify to the fact of the first celebration of Bloomsday.

O'Brien was certainly not idle during the forties and fifties, but he produced nothing of any real substance or note. *An Béal Bocht (The Poor Mouth)* came out in 1941, but it was written in Irish, and though it was rightly recognized as a major work of parody, it necessarily had a very restricted audience. It was not translated until after his death.

In 1943 his play *Faustus Kelly* was performed at the Abbey Theatre in

Dublin. His adaptation of the Čapek brothers' *The Life of Insects* opened at the Gaiety Theatre that same year; O'Brien's version, called *The Insect Play,* was not destined for a long or successful run. He wrote "The Boy from Ballyrearim" in 1955 as a television drama, but it was not produced until 1962, when it appeared in a revised form. Although he wrote several other plays for television and a 15-minute weekly series called "The Ideas of O'Dea," the humor is weak and O'Brien had little conception of the possibilities the medium offered. He does not seem to have enjoyed the experience particularly. "The Ideas of O'Dea" got high viewing ratings, but "it was a miracle that anything reached the screen week after week through the labyrinth of phone calls, cancellation of camera dates, postponements and incompetent fooling of every kind."[44]

At Swim-Two-Birds was republished in 1960, and it generated more interest than it had done in 1939. It was translated into French, and although O'Brien was unstinting in his praise of the translator's work, he still wrote, "I hold that damn book AS2B in the highest detestation and almost blush at the mere mention of it, for it is schoolboy juvenalia."[45] The book became "that old juvenile nightmare of mine AS2B."[46] He was even more scathing and claimed that he could not take the book seriously "on any level and absolutely loathe the mere mention."[47] Yet whatever O'Brien's own feelings, the book has been rightly recognized as a modern classic. For O'Brien it might have represented a youthful and irreverent, high-spirited broadside at narrative conventions and modernist pretentions. But for these very reasons O'Brien's response in writing *At Swim-Two-Birds* can be seen, retrospectively, to sum up spectacularly a particular anarchistic spirit of the age.

It is possible that this republication galvanized him into renewed creative effort, possibly to prove that he could do better—though if that was the intention, he certainly failed. *The Hard Life* came out in 1961. It sold well in Dublin and got good reviews, but O'Brien was uncertain of the British market: "Those people are very hard to amuse—they look for overtones, undertones, subtones, grunts and 'philosophy,' they assume something very serious is afoot. It's disquieting for a writer who is only, for the moment, clowning."[48] Although his mistrust of critics seems here to be focused on national characteristics and directed at the British in particular, he was scornful of critics in general and was certain they were going to misunderstand his next novel, *The Dalkey Archive:* "I have a horrible fear that some stupid critic (and which of them is not?) will praise me as a master of science fiction."[49]

It was as he began work on *The Dalkey Archive* that O'Brien's health began to fail, two separate issues that he felt were linked. He claimed that Saint Augustine, who appears as a character in *The Dalkey Archive*, "had it in" for him because he revealed unpleasant biographical material. O'Brien was fascinated by Augustine, whose youth had been outstanding for its profligacy and carnal wantonness; it is likely that he committed acts of bestiality, and he certainly drank heavily before his conversion to Christianity. These were the details O'Brien was interested in unearthing. "Augustine attracted me in particular," O'Brien remarked, "for in the course of his extended Latin works he heaped obloquy on heresiarchs and voluptuaries, taking care to list and severely castigate his own transgressions."[50]

English, French, and German translations of Augustine's confessions were inadequate for his purpose, because they tended to supress much of the salacious material. Thus O'Brien read all the works in the original Latin, determined to ensure that his facts were accurate. He wanted to "jeer uproariously at Augustine's fleshly obsessions" and felt certain that the saint himself punished him for his painstaking attention to prurient detail.

One night in September 1963, "through an alcoholic nightmare or traumatic spasm" O'Brien fell out of bed and his wife found him unconscious on the floor. He was rushed to the hospital, where at first it was believed he had suffered a heart attack. Subsequent examination showed that in fact he had had a severe attack of uranemia. O'Brien wrote, "How further alerted Augustine had become may be guessed from what happened when I had to travel by bus from my suburban home to the outer edge of Dublin to buy a stamp for an urgent letter. I do not remember leaving the bus on the return trip. A passing motorist found me unconscious at my home stop and later in hospital it was found that my right leg was broken above the ankle. The surgeon was insisting on a bone graft."

Three weeks later he returned home with his leg in plaster from hip to toes, "a terrible nuisance to everybody, including myself." His movement was restricted to the journey between his bed and fireside, which is where he continued writing *The Dalkey Archive*. But his problems were still not over: "Soon I developed sycosis or barber's rash, a disease which I found could only be countered by X-rays such as would make the hairs of the beard temporarily fall out."[51]

Pleurisy and three more weeks in the hospital followed not long after. The theft of manuscripts and files of correspondence from O'Brien's house was a minor disturbance, given the state of his health; the items were recovered by the police from the house of a young man who had taken to visiting O'Brien while he was still immobile. But worse was to happen: "A diversified pain about the left side of the face, present and increasing for about a year, made me seek medical advice about the end of July. A 'specialist' diagnosed neuralgia, a quasi-fictional disease meaning 'nerve-pain.' Later, when I drew attention to a slight 'knottiness' in the neck region, my man said this was a matter for a commoner sort of surgeon." O'Brien was operated on and sent for ray treatment, which in his innocence he at first believed to be simply ultraviolet rays, or something equally innocuous. "Too late," he said, "I realized I was getting what is called deep X-ray therapy, and under a reckless lout of a doctor who exercised no supervision or control. Briefly I was fried alive and, on a tide of vomit, had to enter another hospital to be decarbonized, or 'decoked.'" Inevitably he was anemic and needed regular blood transfusions. Four months before he died, he wrote, "I have not been in my health since I wrote that book or thought of writing it. I thank only Augustine"—and one cannot help feeling that O'Brien was at least half-serious in his belief.[52]

He was, however, supremely confident about his achievement in *The Dalkey Archive*. "It is an unusual book," he wrote to Timothey O'Keeffe; "it will not be lumped together with NEW Novels. . . . Even denunciation of it will have to be individual."[53] The following year, when Hugh Leonard, the playwright, suggested that the book be dramatized, O'Brien agreed to allow him to adapt it, but issued a word of warning: "I take great care with dialogue and would like the style of the book to be preserved."[54] That ominous word *style,* which could have presented any number of difficulties, did not become a bone of contention between novelist and playwright: O'Brien was impressed with Leonard's version. The play opened on 27 September 1965 at the Gate Theatre. O'Brien, not surprisingly, was a guest of honor on the first night. But by this time his health was very poor, and he was taken ill during the performance; he did not see the play in its entirety until November of the same year.

The Dalkey Archive became *The Saints Go Cycling In,* and O'Brien was generous in his praise, not only to Leonard himself but—the true test—when he wrote to other people about Leonard's adaptation: "He seems to have pulled together what in many parts must have seemed like a rather crumpled mattress and produced something solid that has cohesion, coherence and pace, without losing any of the original funny business."[55] O'Brien paid tribute to several ingenious alterations Leonard made to his plot, and in particular to the "smashing final curtain." In a letter to O'Keeffe describing Leonard's ending and comparing it with his own, O'Brien concludes that "this brain wave (and tidal wave) would much improve the book."[56] One might have expected a certain amount of resentment that a book he was proud of writing should, in his opinion, be improved on by somebody else—especially as O'Brien was not particularly well known for possessing a generous nature. Far from showing resentment, however, he seems only to have felt a surprised delight, similar to that he experienced when reading Morisset's inspired translation of his first novel.

O'Brien started another novel, which was to be called *Slattery's Sago Saga,* in 1965. He completed the first seven chapters, but the book was a casualty of his illness and "total stasis" prevailed—he did no work on it after November 1965. He did, however, plan another television series based on the police sergeant from *The Dalkey Archive;* it was to be called "The Detectional Fastidiosities of Sergeant Fottrell." Two weeks before he died, he wrote to Gunnar Rugheimer of the Irish television station about his ideas:

The first mystery adventure is hilarious but in delineating the character and unbelievable virtuosity of the Sergeant, Policeman Pluck must be fully portrayed. In addition to being the dumbest cluck imaginable, he is an amalgam of Frankenstein, Groucho Marx, the Little Flower and President Johnson. In one operation he carries through practically single-handed, he finds the culprit is the Sergeant! Later, when the Sergeant's personality and tongue form a countrywide treasure, the Sergeant may well take a hand in interfering with other people's programmes and ultimately could become the unofficial voice of T. E. [Telefis Eireann]. He would make his remarkable views known on Nelson, the Budget, Decimals . . . anything of current import; he transcends all his situations.[57]

Unfortunately, O'Brien himself did not. Time and money, he said, would have to be found for "Sergeant Fottrell," and he aimed to have the project in production before Christmas—but he was about to go back into the hospital for yet more blood transfusions. From the way he wrote, he gave no indication of his own awareness of just how ill he was: he died on April Fools' Day, 1 April 1966.

Patrick Kavanagh and John Ryan were among the mourners at his funeral. Ryan recalls Kavanagh's story of the last time he saw O'Brien: "When he was lying in bed in hospital, some fella brought him a naggin of gin and a baby tonic. He filled Myles' glass with the entire contents of the gin, adding about half a thimbleful of tonic. "Almighty God," Myles gasped, "Are you trying to drown it entirely?"[58]

Chapter Two

At Swim-Two-Birds

Flann O'Brien and the Modernists

At Swim-Two-Birds is a novel in which the first-person narrator, an incipient novelist, presents us with extracts from his manuscript and descriptions of his life in Dublin. He is a student with a particular interest in literature, and his fiction describes characters who are also engaged in writing or telling stories. This basic structuring of narratives within narratives allows O'Brien ample scope for indulging a talent for widely differing styles: from the compound-word archaisms of the Finn MacCool sections to his pastiche of contemporary best-selling westerns, depending on which of his characters is in charge at the time. The "frame" level of the work can be described as realistic, the youthful narrator firmly located at his university in Dublin, but *At Swim* is a fantasy; various characters from totally incompatible backgrounds meet in the medium of the narrative; different literary genres are thus incongruously brought together; and the Chinese-box narratives within narratives are shown to be less discrete than might be supposed.

O'Brien's comments about the book, in letters to his publishers and to various friends and acquaintances, help to clarify his concerns and go some way toward explaining why *At Swim* is uproariously funny, while being at the same time a difficult book to read. O'Brien sent a copy of it to Ethel Mannin, an established Irish novelist, when it was first published. She was not impressed:

With the best will in the world [I] find I cannot read those Birds (what does the title mean, please, if it means anything?) any more than I can read *Ulysses*. I don't understand this wilful obscurity, & am baffled by G.G.'s [Graham Greene, the publisher's reader] enthusiasm for something so obscure. If it is true as you assert that most novels have been written before and written better, why not leave it that Joyce has done *this* sort of thing before? If one is to imitate why not something that can be understood by one's audience? Its not very difficult to imitate the obscurantists, but not at all easy to imitate shall we say Shakespeare, who was not above making his meaning clear.[1]

Mannin raises many issues central to any critical discussion of *At Swim*. Why should the novel be so "obscure?" Why write at all if the weight of past literature suggests there is nothing new to add? Where does James Joyce fit into the picture? And what *is* the relevance of the title? O'Brien's humor comes out in his reply:

It is a pity you do not like my beautiful book. As a genius, I do not expect to be readily understood but you may be surprised to know that my book is a definite milestone in literature, completely revolutionises the English novel and puts the shallow pedestrian English writers in their place. . . . To be serious, I can't quite understand your attitude to stuff like this. It is not a pale-faced sincere attempt to hold the mirror up and has nothing in the world to do with James Joyce. It is supposed to be a lot of belching, thumb-nosing and belly-laughing and I honestly believe that it is funny in parts. It is also by way of being a sneer at all the slush which has been unloaded from this country on the credulous English. . . . I don't think your dictum about "making your meaning clear" would be upheld in any court of law. You'll look a long time for clear meaning in the Marx Brothers or even Karl Marx. . . . The fantastic title . . . is largely the idea of my old-world publishers. My own title was "Sweeny in the Trees." Search me for the explanation of this wilful obscurity.[2]

Many of O'Brien's typical attitudes are latent in this letter: debunking other literature; insisting that meaning is not transparent; allowing others—in this case his publishers—to make decisions for him, thus including an element of chance; and refusing to explain difficulties. He refutes the Joyce connection. Above all, it is his tone, poised between humor and seriousness, that is typical of his attitude to his own work and to other fiction: Mannin's objections were important enough to be answered, but not addressed with sustained gravity. In other words, literature should be taken seriously, but not too seriously.

O'Brien's reasons for thinking in this way can best be explained by a discussion of Joyce's fiction. The comparison was one that continued to annoy O'Brien throughout his life, in my opinion because critics tended to see him *only* in relation to Joyce—not least because of the shared Dublin background—whereas those tendencies in literature which O'Brien was parodying were much more general. Joyce is, however, an obvious example of modernist traits.

Instead of the classic device of the omnipotent narrator who explains what he thinks we may not understand, indicating as he does so where our sympathies should lie, modernist writers tended to use either multiple or limited narrative perspectives, and relied on myth, literary reference, and allusion in what could be described as an attempt to provide a (relatively) objective basis of common ground for their readers. An underlying allusive structure can be used in an infinite number of ways, but most importantly, if it is sustained, It can provide structure and coherence to the work.

In practice the technique of literary reference and allusion often works to emphasize the difficulties of communication: can any writer expect his audience to share his own particular knowledge of literature, and thus catch every reference? The result is often to underline the isolation and subjective experience of the individual: author, fictional character, and reader. If the reader perseveres and carefully looks up quotations or allusions, he or she will usually eventually find that they work toward some particular end, providing parallel examples from past ages, for instance. Most general readers will need to do a great deal of work before they can catch every nuance intended by the writer, and can admire what may subsequently emerge as aesthetic coherence and organization of the work. It is this new expectation that readers will expend inordinate amounts of time and effort on understanding such a work of fiction that O'Brien mocks in *At Swim*. At the same time he expresses skepticism about the way in which fragments (of experience and of literature, best summarized by T. S. Eliot's line from *The Waste Land* "these fragments I have shored against my ruins") become ordered and cohesive.

Joyce, Eliot, and Woolf might be accused of supreme arrogance because they implicitly assume readers will spend an inordinate amount of time and mental energy in deciphering their work. Joyce was quite open about the matter: "The demand that I make of my reader is that he should devote his whole life to reading my works."[3] Undoubtedly relationships between writers, their texts, and their readers did change in the first decades of the twentieth century. As Virginia Woolf wrote, "All human relationships have shifted—those between masters and servants, husbands and wives, parents and children. And when human relationships change there is at the same time a change in religion, conduct, politics and literature. Let us agree to place one of these changes about the year 1910."[4]

Woolf's famous statement applies to novels and readers too. O'Brien was critical enough of this new application required of readers to mock it, but did so in such a way that overearnest effort on the reader's part is also an object of the mockery. In *At Swim* the reader has no way of knowing whether underlying correspondences between diverse allusions are intended or are purely gratuitous. Research shows that connections *can* be found. They could also be entirely fortuitous. Our uncertainty regarding authorial intention—are connections accident or design?—is O'Brien's criticism of the value that modernist writers placed on aesthetic organization. If patterns and parallels, echoes and resonances can be achieved through randomness, then deliberate choice, made to achieve similar effects, is valueless.

Undoubtedly Joyce was the innovator and experimenter of the era who could not be ignored if one were a student with literary aspirations at college in Dublin in the 1930s. *Finnegans Wake* was published in serial form during those years, keeping Joyce's name before his public. Niall Sheridan, a fellow student of O'Brien's, wrote, "Joyce, of course, was in the very air we breathed."[5] One particular type of literary allusion in *At Swim* is the frequent evocation of Joyce's fiction. It would be possible to contend that the basic setting of the idle but intelligent student's life in Dublin that *A Portrait of the Artist as a Young Man* and *At Swim* share is adventitious, based on necessarily superficial experiences of two writers separated by more than 30 years but living in the same place and attending the same institution. But *At Swim*'s narrator cultivates a stance as the isolated artist, alienated from uncongenial surroundings—a particularly literary pose and one that, because it had its most celebrated antecedent in Joyce's Stephen Dedalus, seems deliberately to invite comparison.

Whatever O'Brien said later to the contrary, the fact that within the novel O'Brien's student explains his own work, "affording an insight as to its aesthetic, its daemon, its argument, its darkness, its sun-twinkle clearness" (25), becomes significant over and above its immediate function as a humorous exposure of "fictional works." It invites comparisons with chapter 5 of *A Portrait,* in which Stephen forces his friend Lynch to listen to his theories of applied Aquinas. Lynch fulfills much the same skeptical role as Brinsley does in *At Swim.* Brinsley's response is "That is all my bum"; Lynch's first reaction is "Stop! I won't listen! I am sick. I was out last night on a yellow drunk with Horan and Goggins."[6] But Stephen is not put off, and Lynch does follow his theories about the nature of beauty, albeit with a certain amount of detachment: " 'Bull's eye again!' said Lynch wittily. 'Tell me now what is *claritas* and you win the cigar.' "[7]

Stephen Dedalus is alienated from family, state, and religion; flees these "nets"; and chooses exile at the end of *A Portrait,* unlike O'Brien's narrator, who is reconciled with his uncle and has no thoughts of leaving Dublin at the end of *At Swim.* In this, the two writers' lives can be said to parallel those of their characters—Joyce went to Paris, returned briefly to Dublin, and spent the rest of his life in Italy, Austria, and France; O'Brien lived all his life in Ireland. Joyce convinces his reader that an essential first step for an artist is to distance himself from his environment, Stephen must be disaffected and autonomous. We read *A Portrait* as if it were the later production of the character Stephen, when he has reached artistic maturity and is able to look back over his early development with detachment.

Stephen is undoubtedly a sensitive young man, and Joyce treats him with irony, but never less than seriousness. The only writing that Stephen actually produces within the novel is the villanelle, deliberately of dubious literary merit because Joyce's whole intention is to show development of the potential artist rather than achievement. O'Brien's protagonist, on the other hand, offers countless examples of his writing.

At Swim appears to have little in common with Joyce's careful structuring, offering instead a kind of patchwork and creating the impression that whatever interested its author at the time had to become part of the text. And so if we think of Joyce as we read *At Swim,* the similarities usually work to show fundamental differences in the two writers' approaches—a good reason in itself for considering Joyce and O'Brien together.

Joyce uses the name "Stephen Dedalus" with great efficacy and economy. Stephen is identified with the martyr saint of that name—Heron "tortures" him, for example—and the director of studies makes the same connection when encouraging Stephen to consider the priesthood. Stephen himself thinks of Stephen's *Green* (a location in Dublin), a color variously associated with creativity and nationalism in the novel. The marriage, then, of his (literally) Christian name with that of a pagan Greek—inventor, artist, craftsman—suggests in microcosm one of the central conflicts of the novel: the pressure of a society that restrains, and the need to assert individuality, to find a personal identity.

Given the significance with which Joyce invests his protagonist's name, we may ask, How positive was O'Brien's decision *not* to name his character? We name things, and people, in order to "know" and thus exert control over them. Countless legends and folktales turn on the hero's need to discover his adversary's name in order to tame or neutralize the adversary's influence. O'Brien's protagonist eludes us because we do not know what to call him. "The protagonist," "the narrator"—whatever words we use are inevitably more clumsy than a name would be. Further, because we need to use these technical terms, our attention is focused on fictional technicalities; we are not allowed to forget that what we have read is largely about constructing a novel. The first-person narrator of *The Third Policeman* is also anonymous, and it is significant that Brian O'Nolan the writer covered his tracks (he thought of using pen names in those terms) by adopting a different name or persona for almost every literary venture he embarked on.

The other main implications of the refusal to name is that O'Brien leaves open the possibility for identification with similar sensitive literary types. The narrator finds his situation uncongenial, but, *At Swim,* unlike *A Portrait,* gives little indication of "nets" for the protagonist to fly. The pose is a truly literary one, the more so because it is without the "realistic" motivation one might expect. This may well be O'Brien's point: his author is a Stephen Dedalus figure (and by not naming, this specific association is encouraged) but he has neither Stephen's potential talent (there is little logic in his literary theory) nor Stephen's reasons for feeling alienated.

There are certainly various passages in *At Swim* that can be read as parodies of episodes not only of *A Portrait* but of *Ulysses.* The Nighttown trial scene in Joyce's "Circle" chapter can be compared with Trellis's trial; "Cyclops" with the compound-word, heroic-catalog style of O'Brien's Finn MacCool sections; and the scientific and impersonal "Ithaca" with the Furriskey, Shanahan, and Lamont pedantry. Undoubtedly O'Brien took advantage of the fact that Joyce's work was well known in his own circle, and thought that his readers would recognize the humor of certain parallels. But *At Swim* is not a consistently purposeful parody of Joyce, and it can be enjoyed without prior knowledge of *A Portrait* or *Ulysses.* What O'Brien was criticizing was obscurity—perhaps in Joyce, certainly in modernist writers—and his criticism took the form of exuberant exaggeration: doing what the modernists tended to do, only more so. His increasing dislike of the Joyce comparison over the years suggests that O'Brien was disappointed his work had been considered *only* in relation to Joyce's, and that other qualities needed consideration. "If I hear that word Joyce again I will surely froth at the gob!"[8] he wrote to O'Keeffe after *At Swim* had been republished.

At O'Brien's request, Sheridan took a copy of *At Swim* to Joyce when he went to Paris in 1939. Sheridan reports that "Joyce greatly enjoyed *At Swim-Two-Birds,* which he considered a comic work of remarkable creative power. (He often complained that too many of the serious commentators on *Ulysses* failed to recognize that it was essentially 'a funny book.')''[9] This remark suggests Joyce was praising in O'Brien an aspect he would like to have had more generally recognized in his own work; it also suggests that he recognized and approved in *At Swim* a less reverent commentary on his own novel than he was used to reading.

Eighteen years separate the publication of *Ulysses* and *At Swim,* and during that time many other "experimental" works appeared. Technical devices common to much of this so-called avant-garde fiction paradoxically (and inevitably) established a self-conscious *orthodoxy,* manifest particularly in the practice of novelists' including novelists in their novels. By introducing an excess of novelists in *At Swim,* O'Brien both mocks and continues the device. James Branch Cabell (an American writer O'Brien read), William Saroyan, and Aldous Huxley had all used this strategy; André Gide's *The Counterfeiters* provides an earlier and more well-known example. O'Brien seems to have been responding to critical questions raised by this kind of experiment—an important point, as it does help to direct attention toward comparisons other than with Joyce. If one's subject is the chaotic and fragmentary modern world, then certainty of a kind can be introduced into one's writing by including a writer in it. This draws attention to the writing process, and the novel almost inevitably becomes self-referential: a closed circuit is established, and reference to the more complicated real world can be ignored or denied. Fiction's subject matter becomes fiction itself. But in O'Brien's hands, there is an excess. His writer-narrator has a novelist in his fiction, and in turn *his* characters take over the writing. Such excesses provide an anarchic energy, an overdetermined self-reference that, far from providing a secure framework for the reader, deliberately confuses.

Literary Reference and Quotation

In the opening paragraph the narrator reflects, appropriately enough, on ways of beginning a novel: "One beginning and one ending for a book was a thing I did not agree with. A good book may have three openings entirely dissimilar and inter-related only in the prescience of the author, or for that matter one hundred times as many endings." His interests are quite clearly with experiment, rather than more traditional realism. Three examples of openings follow (though of course the book has already opened with the narrator's thoughts), each introducing a character from the narrator's manuscripts who will appear again later: the Pooka MacPhillimey, Mr. John Furriskey, and Finn MacCool, "a legendary hero of old Ireland." These diverse characters are supposed to be the creations

of Dermot Trellis (the novelist the narrator has invented), as we learn
later:

Synopsis, being a summary of what has gone before, FOR THE BENEFIT OF NEW
READERS: Dermot Trellis, an eccentric author, conceives the project of writing a
salutary book on the consequences which follow wrong-doing and creates for the
purpose
        The Pooka Fergus MacPhellimey, a species of human Irish devil endowed
with magical powers. He then creates
        John Furriskey, a depraved character, whose task is to attack women and
behave at all times in an indecent manner. . . .
        Finn MacCool, a legendary character hired by Trellis on account of the
former's venerable appearance and experience.(61)[10]

When Virginia Woolf introduces a writer or artist figure into her novels
(Lily Briscoe in *To the Lighthouse,* Bernard in *The Waves,* Miss La Trobe in
Between the Acts, even the eponymous Orlando wrestling with poetry), she
has particular aesthetic points to make; the writer's or artist's struggle and
achievement have a direct bearing on the integrity of the text as a whole.
In *Point Counter Point* Aldous Huxley's character Philip Quarles says that
putting a novelist into a novel justifies aesthetic generalizations. Trellis,
the narrator-novelist's novelist, has none of these functions. He is an
excuse for O'Brien's humor.
        At a time when this self-referential device was being used to raise
critical and aesthetic consciousness about the role of the artist, Trellis is
anachronistic and anomalous, concerned with "sin and the wages
attaching thereto," not artistic matters: "He is appalled by the spate of
sexual and other crimes recorded in recent times in the newspapers. . . .
[He] wants this salutary book to be read by all. He realizes that a purely
moralizing tract would not reach the public. Therefore he is putting
plenty of smut into his book. There will be no less than seven indecent
assaults on young girls and any amount of bad language" (35). Which is
how the narrator describes Trellis to his friend Brinsley. Undoubtedly and
intentionally Trellis has severe (and comic) limitations: "All colors except
green he regarded as symbols of evil and he confined his reading to books
attired in green covers. Although a man of wide learning and culture, this
arbitrary rule caused serious chasms in his erudition. The Bible, for
instance, was unknown to him" (99).
        But Trellis does share one important characteristic with more serious
writers of the time: his fiction refers constantly to the work of other
writers, and in fact most of his characters "are characters used in other

books, chiefly the work of another great writer called Tracy." O'Brien, whose own book could be described as a montage of extracts from both popular and obscure preexisting publications, in this instance raises the issue of plagiarism. He takes intertextuality to what seems to be a logical conclusion and willfully reduces it to passing off someone else's work as one's own.

In a court scene Trellis is charged with plagiarism: "I put it to you that the passage was written by Mr. Tracey and that you stole it" (42). Trellis denies the charge, and the matter is left unresolved as the questioning reaches ever more ludicrous heights. But quotation, reference, and allusion are fundamental to the whole novel, and it is significant that Trellis the writer is also a reader, one who has "serious chasms", like the Bible, in his reading. In his "aesthetic," the narrator holds that "[t]he modern novel should be largely a work of reference. Most authors spend their time saying what has been said before—usually said much better. A wealth of references to existing works would acquaint the reader instantaneously with the nature of each character, would obviate tiresome explanations and would effectively preclude mountebanks, upstarts, thimbleriggers and persons of inferior education from an understanding of contemporary literature" (25). And up to a point, he pursues this policy in his manuscript. It is significant that although the narrator has the works of "Mr. Joyce" on his washstand (11) the Joyce allusions are O'Brien's: it is in the person of the narrator himself that Stephen Dedalus is brought to mind. Eager to avoid the charge of plagiarism, or perhaps to be fair to his readers, the narrator always gives precise details of his sources whenever he quotes and incorporates someone else's material into his own manuscript. One of the best examples of this practice is the way in which he characterizes Trellis.

The narrator and his friend Brinsley have been discussing the narrator's manuscript, and are interrupted by the narrator's uncle. When he leaves the room, Brinsley remarks, "I hope . . . that Trellis is not a replica of the uncle." The narrator says, "I did not answer but reached a hand to the mantelpiece and took down the twenty-first volume of my *Conspectus of the Arts and Natural Sciences.* Opening it, I read a passage which I subsequently embodied in my manuscript as being suitable for my purpose. The passage had in fact reference to Dr. Beatty (now with God) but boldly I took it for my own" (30).

The narrator does, however, preface the quotation with a heading, *"Extract from 'A Conspectus of the Natural Arts and Sciences,' being a description of Trellis's person,"* a practice he follows whenever he quotes,

which he frequently does, from this encyclopedia. Thus, there should be
no accusation of plagiarism attaching to his use of the "wealth of
references to existing works" (25). But the matter is not so simple. For
the narrator, the *Conspectus* is real, and from it he takes quotations from
the eighteenth-century poets Falconer and Cowper.

But it is difficult to determine whether the *Conspectus* was equally real
for O'Brien. Certainly all the extracts are genuine and can be traced to
their sources: Beatty (whose name is actually spelled "Beattie") was an
eighteenth-century poet and philosopher; the narrator's extract comes
from Alexander Dyce's "Memoir of James Beattie."[11] Falconer's "The
Shipwreck," which appears toward the end of *At Swim* (210ff.), was
published many times. The *"description of how a day may be spent, being an
extract from 'A Conspectus of the Arts and Natural Sciences,' from the hand of
Mr. Cowper,"* incorporated into the narrator's manuscript on page 149 of
At Swim, can be found in an edition of Cowper's letters—it was written
in Huntingdon on 20 October 1766. Determining the authenticity of
these extracts requires a great deal of research, however, for the narrator's
source, the *Conspectus,* is not to be found in any library catalog. It does not
appear in the British Library catalog or in the National Union catalog,
and it is not in bibliographers' manuals of English literature. This is not
to say that it certainly never existed, but it is clear that citing the work as a
source is virtually useless for the earnest reader who, having learned new
techniques by reading (for example) *The Waste Land,* looking up all the
references that appear in the notes Eliot appended, and thereby grasping
the extent (though not necessarily the significance!) of literary reference in
that poem, might fondly believe the same method can be applied to *At
Swim-Two-Birds.*

Most homes possess encyclopedias; children are taught to look things
up in them; they are familiar. But few homes will own the same
publication, and the chances of O'Brien's reader having a *Conspectus* on
hand is one of his jokes against the increasingly intense business of literary
criticism and scholarship. It is one of *At Swim's* many paradoxes that
those "forty buckskin volumes" which *sound* so accessible, because we all
recognize that particular type of publication, resist all efforts to trace
them. The general reader who enjoys *At Swim* without stopping to wonder
whether these quotations are genuine or invented by O'Brien remains free
from his laughter. The scholar intent on looking up each reference in
order to understand its bearing on the work as a whole is the butt of his
joke.

James Beattie was famous in his day, but unless one specializes in the eighteenth century, even the student of literature is unlikely to have come across him. O'Brien intensifies this obscurity by quoting not from one of Beattie's poems but from a memoir written after his death that seems to have very little application to *At Swim*. Dr. Beattie was a real person, but mention of his name does not "acquaint the reader instantaneously" with the nature of what Trellis's character is supposed to be. The dedicated researcher will discover that Beattie's wife suffered from insanity, which fact forced him to live apart from her; that Beattie was deeply concerned that his two sons might inherit their mother's madness; but that in fact both boys died of consumptive diseases at ages 18 and 22. Madness becomes a theme in *At Swim*—Trellis is goaded into losing his mind when the fictional characters he has created get out of hand and begin torturing him. Beattie's sons' weak chests may well be echoed in the narrator's concern for his own pulmonary well-being: "a congenital disposition predisposing me to the most common of wasting diseases—a cousin had died in Davos" (44). But neither madness nor consumption is evident in O'Brien's quotation from Dyce's memoir, without a great deal of background research.

This omission poses a problem. Any literary reference or allusion is an important indication of the author's assumptions about his ideal reader. The author envisages his reader as one who will recognize the original he quotes from, refers to, or parodies, and also assumes that the reader will have the wit to see the application to his own work. In *To the Lighthouse*, for example, Woolf quotes from Cowper, but her quotation comes from a poem, "The Castaway" (which has more public currency than O'Brien's quotation from one of Cowper's letters), and does so in a way that unmistakably reinforces her characterization of Mr. Ramsay. Verses from "The Castaway" are put into his mouth and by association add to his self-dramatizing nature—Cowper wrote in extremity, beside which Ramsay's doubts are unimportant. Woolf, of course, expects her readers to share this intertextual knowledge; she certainly does not cite sources, either in footnotes or within her text. The purpose of her quotation, unlike that of O'Brien's, is clear. Similarly, Joyce's *Hamlet* references in *Ulysses* are both pervasive and fully integrated. If by explicitly citing his sources in emphatic italics O'Brien intends to ridicule the tendency— present in Woolf, Joyce, Eliot, and others—to assume in readers an increasingly large working knowledge of a vast range of literature, then we must ask why his sources are so obscure and the evidence so misleadingly presented. The answer, surely, is that he is intent on poking fun at the critical industry that was beginning to grow up around these modernist writers.

The *Athenian Oracle* is quoted only once in *At Swim,* but although its existence can be proved—the extracts that appear on page 102 of *At Swim* come from volume 2, published in 1704—it has little bearing on O'Brien's work beyond that of sheer pleasure in (what now seems) the ludicrousness of the questions posed: "Woman, is it possible for her to conceive when asleep?" or "Horse, with a round fundament, why does it emit a square excrement?" The *"Extract from Literary Reader, the Higher Class, by the Irish Christian Brothers"* (21) also has a verifiable, though obscure existence, and was not invented by O'Brien, but again, the reader has no way of knowing this. The main reason for its inclusion seems to have been delight in its style: "And in the flowers that wreathe the sparkling bowl, fell adders hiss and poisonous serpents roll—Prior. What is alcohol? All medical authorities tell us it is a double poison—an irritant and a narcotic poison. . . . The lungs, being overtaxed, become degenerated, and this is why so many inebriates suffer from a peculiar form of consumption . . . many, many cases of which, are, alas to be found in our hospitals where the unhappy victims await the slow but sure march of an early death" (21).

The inclusion of passages from the *Athenian Oracle,* the Christian Brothers' reader, the biblical apocryphal book of Ecclesiasticus, and the *Conspectus* suggests randomness. If they were indeed carefully chosen, the thought behind that choice was deliberately intended to force the overearnest scholar into the most ingenious subtextual readings—a gibe at the post–James Joyce critical industry.

Randomness, Organization, and First-Person Narrative

Randomness itself can be seen as a protest against the careful aesthetic structuring of such works as *Ulysses* and *To the Lighthouse.* This can be shown by examining other parts of *At Swim,* parts that may not be immediately apparent as quotations. The evidence for this rests largely on the testimony of Niall Sheridan, O'Brien's contemporary at University College who became Brinsley in the novel. In a memoir written after O'Brien's death, Sheridan says: "[O'Brien] could write quickly when a theme absorbed him and soon he began to show me sections of the book as it progressed, explaining the *rationale* behind each episode and its place in the overall design. Very soon, these sections began to form part of the text, and I found myself (under the name of Brinsley) living a sort of double life at the autobiographical core of a work which was in the process of creation."[12]

Brinsley in the book certainly acts as a sounding board for the narrator. His praise is often grudgingly given, and his adverse comments allow the narrator to defend his work. As Brinsley in the novel he exercises his critical judgment, literally helping to create the world of the novel as he reads, and yet he remains subject to the author's ultimate jurisdiction, becoming not only fixed but fictional. According to Sheridan, in real life he advised O'Brien that the completed manuscript, about 800 typewritten pages, was too long, and suggested it should be cut before it was sent to publishers. O'Brien replied, "I am sick of the sight of it. What about cutting it yourself?"[13] Sheridan, it seems, edited it by about one-fifth before it went to Longmans. If you allow your friend to work on your manuscript, you ensure a certain amount of impersonality in your work; but if, as O'Brien did, you also allow your friends to contribute interesting documents to your manuscript, you ensure that chance will play an even greater part. "Chance," or "randomness," is, however, being used as part of a purposeful experiment. O'Brien's method with found (or given) material was undoubtedly similar to his method with quotation and reference. He chose—and thus presumably also rejected—material that he would include. The tipster's letter (12) and the safety-first rules copied from the back of an exercise book (207) are included not because they are examples of excellence in literature, far from it. But both offer individual, idiosyncratic use of language and add to the widely differing styles that constitute the novel as a whole.

The first edition of *At Swim-Two-Birds* began with the heading "Chapter One." When Penguin bought out the first paperback edition, this heading was omitted, presumably because Penguin decided it was an error, as there are no further chapter divisions in the book. A structure of a kind is imposed on the text, however, by 10 "Biographical Reminiscences" that occur at irregular intervals and generally lead into passages of the narrator's manuscript. In the biographical passages the narrator usually mentions the season, and so we can infer that the actual time span of the novel is roughly a year, from one summer to the next. It is the student's final year at the university, and though by his own account he is not addicted to studying, he passes his examinations with "a creditable margin of honor" (208) at the end of the book. The biographical reminiscences are themselves punctuated with various italicized headings; there are, for example, five *"Descriptions of my uncle,"* which are sometimes read as demonstrating a narrative change of heart, though it is difficult to argue this point convincingly. The first such description presents an unprepossessing portrait: "Red-faced, bead-eyed, ball-bellied. Fleshy about the shoulders with long swinging arms giving ape-like effect to gait. Large moustache. Holder of Guinness clerkship the third class" (10). The second concentrates on his nature rather than physical appearance: *"Description of my uncle:* Rat-brained, cunning, concerned-that-he-should-be-well-thought-of. Abounding in pretence, deceit. Holder of Guinness clerkship the third class" (30).

Two more descriptions reiterate these features, but the final one, which comes toward the end, after the student has passed his exams and his uncle has presented him with a gold watch to mark his pleasure in the achievement, produces a kindlier response: *"Description of my uncle:* Simple, well-intentioned; pathetic in humility; responsible member of large commercial concern" (215). By the narrator's own account, the uncle's gesture induces in his nephew an emotion "of surprise and contrition extremely difficult of literary rendition or description." His plan had been to confound his uncle with his success. Throughout, he has been accused of idleness and of wasting the money his father has invested in his education. But his moment of ungenerous triumph is denied, and the wind taken out of his sails, for the uncle has already discovered his result: " 'I've said many a hard word to you for your own good,' he said. 'I have rebuked you for lazyness and bad habits of one kind or another. But you've done the trick . . . and your old uncle is going to be the first to shake your hand. And happy he is to do it' " (213).

The change in the narrator's view of his uncle is not particularly creditable to him, as it is entirely dependent on the uncle's generosity of spirit, not his own—indeed the narrator even rather unkindly points out to the reader that the watch is a secondhand one, and emphasizes this fact by adding, *"Comparable word used by the German nation:* antiquarisch." Nevertheless, his steps do "falter"—presumably from emotion—as he returns to his room. It is still difficult to interpret this as a deliberate departure on O'Brien's part from Joyce's ending of *A Portrait.* Anne Clissmann argues that because Stephen renounces family, state, and religion, O'Brien's protagonist, by contrast, must be reconciled.[14] Un-doubtedly the narrator's final words in this last biographical section indicate that he looks at his watch and at the same time "hears the Angelus pealing out from far away"—and this gesture may be one toward acceptance not only of family but also of the church. Yet his character is shallow, swayed for the moment by his uncle's unexpected gift. There is no indication that the feeling will be sustained—this not least because the novel does not end here, and when it does end, the ending is neither traditional nor conventional. The *"Conclusion of the book, penultimate"* partly resolves the Trellis sections, and it could be marshaled in the argument for a new and more generous spirit; but the *"Conclusion of the book, ultimate"* introduces a narrative voice that has not been heard before, and the mental states it describes are far from being reconciled with anything: the last words of the book are a suicide's farewell.

The narrator's attitude to his fictional character Trellis certainly seems to change in the extract from his manuscript that follows the final biographical reminiscence. In the previous manuscript extract, before he passed his exams, he was engaged in writing about Trellis's torture at the hands of Furriskey, Shanahan, and Lamont. After the gift of the watch, he effects a rescue.

Shanahan and company are Trellis's characters who have quite literally "taken on a life of their own" and bitterly resent the way in which their author manipulates them. They therefore keep him sedated so that they can be self-determining. They are, however, concerned that Trellis may become immune to the drugs they administer. And so when they discover that Orlick, another of their company, has a talent for writing that equals his "father" Trellis's, they suggest that Orlick, to escape authorial despotism, utilize his gift for literary composition by writing scenes in which Trellis is tortured.

There can only have been one previous character called Orlick in fiction, the sinister young man in Dickens's *Great Expectations* who clobbers Mrs. Joe Gargery over the head, relieving her of her senses, though not quite killing her. O'Brien's Orlick serves a similar function in *At Swim*. He is unwilling to kill Trellis—though he is open to persuasion from the others.

Under Orlick's authorship, Trellis, "wind-quick, eye-mad, with innumerable boils upon his back and upon various parts of his person, flew out in his sweat-wet night-shirt and day-drawers, out through the glass of the window till he fell with a crap on the cobbles of the street. A burst eye-ball, a crushed ear and bone-breaks two in number, these were the agonies that were his lot as a result of his accidental fall" (176). Trellis is obliged to stand trial—and Orlick, under instructions from the others, is about to finish him off with a razor. Orlick is concerned about killing their own author: "I only hope that nothing will happen to us. I don't think the like of this has been done before" (208). But the manuscript finishes at this point, with the company poised over the exercise book in which Orlick has been writing.

The antepenultimate conclusion, the "Biographical reminiscence part the final," follows. We learn about the narrator's success and find that he has changed his mind about his uncle. The Angelus peals and the next section, "Conclusion of the book penultimate," returns to the manuscript to rescue Trellis by means of his servant Teresa.

She tidies his room, and in the process picks up several pieces of paper and puts them on the fire: "By a curious coincidence as a matter of fact strange to say it happened that these same pages were those of the master's novel which made and sustained the existence of Furriskey and his true friends" (215–16). She is interrupted by a knock on the door and goes downstairs to admit Trellis, who is still barefoot and in his nightshirt—precisely as he fell from his window in Orlick's manuscript.

The implication is that Teresa has saved Trellis's life by destroying his tormentors and that the narrator-nephew has allowed this situation to happen because of his newfound disposition toward his uncle. Trellis is not absolutely restored to health; the narrator is not quite that magnanimous: "I am ill, Teresa, [Trellis] murmured. I have done too much thinking and writing, too much work. My nerves are troubling me. I have bad nightmares and queer dreams and I walk when I am very tired" (216). "You could easily get your death, Sir" Teresa replies—closer to the truth of Orlick's manuscript than she is aware.

One illusion of the narratives within narratives that texts like O'Brien's produce is the sense that the frame narrative, in this case the narrator's biography, is more realistic than the other sections that make up the whole text. The passages from the narrator's manuscript that deal with Finn MacCool or the Pooka and the Good Fairy are clearly fantasy, whereas the narrator's rather dingy life is, by comparison, realistic. But O'Brien's point was that whatever style he employed in whatever part of his book was precisely that: a style of writing. Each extract is as fictional as any other. The opening of *At Swim* establishes our relationship with the narrator because he addresses us in the first person: "Having placed in my mouth sufficient bread for three minutes' chewing, I withdrew my powers of sensual perception and retired into the privacy of my own mind. . . . I reflected on the subject of my spare-time literary activities. One beginning and one ending for a book was a thing I did not agree with. A good book may have three openings entirely dissimilar and inter-related only in the prescience of the author, or for that matter one hundred times as many endings."

This first paragraph tells us several things about the narrator; there is no physical description of him, but his language and his actions suggest a nature governed by pedantry. A studied, languid sophistication may be detected, with a certain self-consciousness about the impression he is making. We also learn that he is interested in literature and that his leanings are to the avant-garde. He goes on to give us examples of three openings for a novel—and certainly with the antepenultimate, penultimate, and ultimate conclusion he gives us three endings.

If the opening of a novel establishes our relationship with a first-person narrator, then the conclusion is the obvious place to judge how that relationship has developed. Conventionally the last chapters of novels tie up loose ends of plots and perhaps look forward to the future; nineteenth-century novelists in particular anticipate and answer questions readers might ask if they could. At the end of first-person narratives the reader is often addressed directly, as if a formal leave-taking or acknowledgment of the end of a relationship is felt to be a requirement. Dickens's Esther Summerson in *Bleak House,* for example, takes her leave with warmth and affection appropriate to the emotional scenes she has recalled for us: "The few words that I have to add to what I have written are soon penned; then I and the unknown friend to whom I write, will part for ever. Not without much dear remembrance on my side. Not without some, I hope, on his or hers."[15] The last pages of *At Swim* glance at such traditional expectations raised by conclusions like that, but typically O'Brien refuses to gratify them. The last (very long) paragraph of the book begins with the familiar italicized heading that we recognize as the narrator's: *"Conclusion of the book, ultimate,"* but although certain themes of the novel recur in what follows—truth is an odd number, Sweeny in the trees, madness—they are not gathered together in such a way that we may perceive a pattern. Further, we would be hard put to identify the last narrative voice as that of the student narrator. If it is intended to be his, he has adopted an impersonal style different from that in the biographical "penultimate" conclusion and in his manuscript's "antepenultimate" ending.

Among O'Brien's papers at Southern Illinois University is a letter purporting to be from Michael Byrne, who describes himself as "Painter, Poet, Pianist, Composer" in the manner of the character Michael Byrne in O'Brien's *At Swim* (96).[16] The letter takes the form of an invoice and is quite clearly intended as a joke, but among other things it charges O'Brien one shilling for "spare endings for Novel 'At Swim-Two-Birds,' 2 at 6d each." It may well be that O'Brien actually did use "Michael

Byrnes's" "[s]pecially selected pathological (schizophrenic) anecdotes of literary interest, from private case book"—as the invoice goes on to describe them. Whether or not this is the case, a final leave-taking between reader and narrator is avoided. *At Swim* could not end more conclusively, but there is a world of difference between the farewell of one of Dickens's or Charlotte Brontë's narrators and the "good-bye" of O'Brien's.

A man's obsession with the number 3 is initially presented as amusing and trivial in its irrelevance; casually, however, the sentence proceeds to introduce much more serious implications: he "drank three cups of tea with three lumps of sugar in each, cut his jugular with a razor three times and scrawled with a dying hand on a picture of his wife good-bye, good-bye, good-bye." It hardly needs to be said that this is no conventional deathbed novel ending!

Among other things, *At Swim* mocks conventional reader/narrator/ protagonist relationships by bringing them just sufficiently to the reader's consciousness for him or her to be aware of a lack. Close identification with the protagonist is denied. He is an unprepossessing youth, and his namelessness makes him difficult to locate, as it encourages the reader to confuse him with both author and stock literary figure. His namelessness also makes him difficult to refer to. The novel resists our attempts to understand it through our customary complex but effortlessly achieved pretense that we are dealing with and trying to understand a real personality.

Throughout the book O'Brien playfully questions and considers our too-easy assumptions about the way in which life—experience—is turned into fiction. The *"Extract from Manuscript, being a description of a social evening at the Furriskey household"* (150) reads like an extended parody, or fictional account, of earlier social occasions in the uncle's house that were described in the sixth and seventh biographical reminiscences. It is important to remember that although we seem to be watching a writer practicing his craft, both accounts are equally fictitious.

Characterization

The uncle brings his friend Mr. Corcoran home for the evening to listen to an ancient gramophone recording of Gilbert and Sullivan's *Patience*. Both men have "indifferent voices of the baritone range" and are members of the chorus in the Rathmines and Rathgar choir. Listening to the record, they join in the chorus, "in happy and knowledgeable harmony, stressing the beat with manual gesture. My uncle, his back to me, also moved his head authoritatively, exercising a roll of fat he was accustomed to wear at the back of his collar, so that it paled and reddened in the heat of the music" (95). This passage is from a biographical— supposedly realistic—section of the book, but the narrator's minute observation of his uncle's appearance tips the narrative into the realms of the surreal. The phrase that describes the location of the fat suggests that, had he wished, the uncle might have worn it absolutely anywhere about his person. The uncle, as solid and conventional a character as any in fiction, is rendered fantastic by the means his nephew employs to describe him.

Music is also the main subject of conversation at the Furriskeys' social evening. Mrs. Furriskey knows her place and is suitably silent most of the time, but the male members of the gathering are concerned to show their wit and wisdom. In fact, they give a fine demonstration of garbled knowledge imperfectly apprehended. Homer is confused with Socrates, and has the persecution of the Christians attributed to him; Paganini is referred to as Pegasus; Beethoven's Kreuzer Sonata becomes the "Crutch" —of such surpassing beauty that it "makes you tap the shoe leather off your feet."

The "conversationalists" have an intuitive feel for rhetoric: "The voice was first, Furriskey was saying. The human voice. The voice was Number One. Anything that came after was only an imitation of the voice" (150). Lamont, another guest, counters by championing the fiddle, but both characters recognize the sheer power of bludgeoning the opposition with repetition. "But the fiddle, continued Furriskey slow and authoritative of articulation, the fiddle comes number two to the voice" (151). The word *articulation* betrays the nonobjective reporting of this conversation by suggesting a contrast with *articulate,* which Furriskey certainly is not.

The uncle and his friends in the biographical section have a similar discussion on music and dancing for a ceilidhe (a social gathering) they are organizing. They are concerned that they offend neither clergy nor Gaelic League, but Mr. Connors wants to include a waltz in the program: "One old-time waltz is all I ask. It's as Irish as any of them, nothing foreign about the old-time waltz." Mr. Corcoran is not in favor of the idea but begins his objection with two positives: "Oh, yes. Old-time waltzes. Yes. I don't agree with the old-time waltz at all. Nothing *wrong* with it, of course, Mr. Connors, nothing actually *wrong* with it." His speech becomes more repetitive and his metaphors confused as he continues: "But after all a Ceilidhe is not the place for it, that's all. A Ceilidhe is a Ceilidhe. I mean, we have our own. We have plenty of our own dances without crossing the road to borrow what we can't wear. See the point? It's alright, but it's not for us. Leave the waltz to the jazz-boys. By God they're welcome to it as far as I'm concerned" (133).

Robert Adams's description of the dialogue in *At Swim* as "maundering, moronic, and accurate to the last curl of a cliché"[17] is just but gives no indication of the way the narrative qualifies our response to the dialogue. O'Brien does not simply transcribe Dublin idiom. When Brinsley criticizes this portion of the manuscript his objections are conventional; he "expressed his inability to distinguish between Furriskey, Lamont and Shanahan, bewailed what he termed their spiritual and physical identity, stated that true dialogue is dependent on conflict rather than the confluence of two minds and made reference to the importance of characterization in contemporary works of a high-class, advanced or literary nature. The three of them, he said, might make one man between them" (160ff.).

Brinsley's expectations are traditional and nonexperimental, whereas in the exceptional stiffness of both dialogue and narrative, the narrator is exploring the conventions of language. Thus, when Furriskey displays his superior knowledge on the subject of "pianofortes," Lamont asks whether it is wrong to call the instrument simply a "piano": "His attitude was one of civil perplexity; his eyelids fluttered and his lower lip drooped as he made the enquiry" (152). The men do not argue the point: "By virtue of enlightenment, culture and a spirit of give-and-take, the matter was amicably settled to the satisfaction of all parties" (153). This narrative language, in its overly minute description of Lamont's facial expression and legalistic comment on the agreement, is deliberately inappropriate to the situation.

Brinsley is right in one respect: dialogue does suggest engagement. And partly out of politeness the members of the company fail to engage in their usual argumentative way. It is true to say that this section of *At Swim,* together with the description of the social evening at the uncle's that precedes it, might well have not existed without Joyce's prior example of Dubliners' speech. But like Joyce, O'Brien did much more than simply transcribe the conversation and idiom of the drinking population for their own sake. Both writers may represent these elements as "moronic" and "maundering" at times, but both offer dual perspectives. Joyce represents the speech of Dubliners and simultaneously creates the artificial aesthetic worlds of his short stories, wherein no word is extraneous, wherein language is seen to be common but also fulfills an imagistic role within the self-contained world of the story. In O'Brien's case, we are shown the so-called raw material of the uncle's social evening reworked as fiction—the joke being that both are equally fictional, O'Brien's invention, not the narrator's experience and fictional rendering.

O'Brien's use of common speech teaches us not to trust language, and ultimately fiction, including his own. When commonplace verbal conversation is represented in print on a page, a transformation occurs. Metaphors such as "water on the knee is a bad man," "he was a terrible drink of water," and "paralysis is a nice cup of tea" take on a surreal quality, partly encouraged by the language of the narrative passages, which does not work to heighten a sense of reality. For example, the sentence "A sugar bowl containing sugar was passed deftly from hand to hand in the pause" suggests that nothing must be taken for granted, that a sugar bowl being handed to people drinking tea could contain absolutely anything. Similarly, "There was a pleased pause in which the crockery, unopposed, clinked merrily" (153) implies that the tea things have a life of their own, independent of the guests.

In a similar way, intangibles—thought and laughter in particular— are treated as if they were concrete: "A small laugh was initiated and gently circulated" (151); "A laugh was interposed neatly, melodiously, retrieved with skill and quietly replaced" (155), "a privy laugh, orderly and undertoned, was offered and accepted in reward" (159). This practice is not restricted to the "manuscript" extract; the narrator uses the same technique in the biographical section. At the committee meeting after Mr. Connors tells a joke, "there was general acclamation and amusement in which I *inserted* perfunctorily my low laugh" (137); my italics).

Mrs. Furriskey, trying to remember where she saw the blind beggarman (one cannot help thinking it must have been in *Ulysses,* that he is one and the same as Joyce's blind stripling), "rummages with a frown in the interior of her memory" as if her mind were a remnant counter. Having finished with it, "curiously examining it, she replaced her reminiscence" (156).

Description of this kind in this quantity provides a nonrealistic background for the dialogue, making it more preposterous. This aspect, however, is one Brinsley fails to notice, attuned as he is (in this instance) to conventional criticism and concerned only with successful—or unsuccessful—characterization. The narrator defends himself against Brinsley's charges: "Your objections are superficial. These gentlemen may look the same but actually they are profoundly dissimilar."

Typically, his reasons have no apparent bearing on the manuscript Brinsley has just read. "For example," the narrator continues,

Mr. Furriskey is of the brachycephalic order, Mr. Shanahan of the prognathic.
  —Prognathic?
  I continued in this strain in an idle perfunctory manner, searching in the odd corners of my mind where I was accustomed to keep words which I rarely used [very like Mrs. Furriskey's thought processes!]. I elaborated the argument with the aid of dictionaries and standard works of reference, embodying the results of my researches in a memorandum which is now presented conveniently for the information of the reader. (161)

The reader is presented with something that is neither convenient nor informative. The respective "diacritical traits or qualities of Messrs Furriskey, Lamont and Shanahan" that the narrator lists mocks the whole notion of characterization in fiction, and incidentally lampoons fan magazines that list stage and screen stars' favorite things—as if such information were capable of conveying anything personal or even pertinent about anybody, either a rock star's persona as created by a record company or a character in a novel:

Fabric of shirt: tiffany; linen; tarlatan.
Pedal traits: hammer toes; nil; corns.
Favorite flower: camomile; daisy; betony.
Favorite shrub: deutzia; banksia; laurastinus.
Favorite dish: loach; caudle; julienne. (161)

Tables of information like this one, though relatively easy to consult for reference, are alien to the whole concept of novel reading. They are difficult to assimilate and harder to recall. Beckett uses a similar technique in *Murphy* for describing Celia. He lists various physical attributes and gives a brief description, in most cases a simple measurement, for each:

Upper arm 11″   Wrist 6″
Forearm $9\frac{1}{2}$″   Bust 34″[18]

If the reader collates this information, which runs to twenty facts, he will discover that Celia conforms to an ideal of feminine perfection as promoted by advertising agencies, an ideal that is generally considered highly acceptable. But figures on the page in this tabular form primarily convey messages about the kind of novel *Murphy* is; only as a secondary consideration do they describe Celia. The sentence that follows the list, "She stormed away from the callbox, accompanied delightfully by her hips," undoubtedly has surreal qualities, but it also implies a great deal more about Celia's physical appearance and movements than the careful (invented) measurements—down to the last quarter of an inch—that preceded it.

O'Brien's list, with reference to the narrator's characters, is quite meaningless. However one looks at it, this list, like Beckett's, is an affront to a novel reader's expectations. Lamont's mannerisms, "tooth-sucking and handling of tie knot," could be used in such a way as to "bring him to life." In Virginia Woolf's *Mrs. Dalloway,* for example, Peter Walsh continually fingers his pocket knife, a gesture that gains symbolic significance during the course of the novel. Lamont could have been seen nervously sucking his teeth and perpetually straightening his tie—had O'Brien been writing a novel in which gestures were intended to reflect inner tensions. Instead he aims to send up modern fictional devices as well as more traditional ones. The narrator's point is exactly this, that his detailed information adds nothing to the extract that we—and Brinsley —have just read. It is an irrelevance, and yet such is the narrator's delight in irrelevancies that he plunders dictionaries and "standard works of reference" in order to compile it.

Brinsley's objections to the "social evening" extract seem to point out a limitation in the narrator's skills; but instead of denying the grounds of this criticism by suggesting (as I have) that its true interest lies elsewhere, in an uneasy representation of reality, the narrator delights in taking up this new challenge—rather as he did when Brinsley hoped that the description of Trellis was not a fictional rendering of the uncle, much earlier in the book. On that occasion, the narrator wordlessly reached for his *Conspectus* and used the description of Dr. Beatty to refute the suggestion. Brinsley's is the voice of conventional criticism that works from the principle that fiction aims to represent life. The narrator contradicts this view not by argument but by example, indicating what a meaningless proposition it is to work from if taken literally. Still, it must be said that when O'Brien chooses, Brinsley becomes adept at recognizing and collating motif; his skill as critic and reader is adapted to the needs of the novel, rather than to the kind of consistent fictional character O'Brien had little interest in developing.

In neither instance are Brinsley's objections used in a straightforward manner to help shape the reader's understanding of the narrator's avant-garde aims. Brinsley voices objections that readers may feel, but the narrator, instead of defending and explaining his methods, deftly complicates matters: in each case his refutation by example raises new critical questions—however implicitly—and far from encouraging readers to reconsider (say) the tea-party scene as an exercise in the nonrepresentational properties of language when it is self-consciously employed, diverts our attention to the next problem.

Use of Irish Myth and Legend

Owing to the extraordinary lack of rules that O'Brien and his narrator are willing to observe, Finn MacCool, legendary hero of Old Ireland, is able to coexist with contemporary characters in *At Swim*. Finn is introduced on the first page as an example of "the third opening" of the novel: "Though not mentally robust, he was a man of superb physique and development. Each of his thighs was as thick as a horse's belly, narrowing to a calf as thick as the belly of a foal. Three fifties of fosterlings could engage with handball against the wideness of his backside, which was large enough to halt the march of men through a mountain-pass." There were several cycles of early Irish tales, but those which lent themselves to burlesque or "humorous fantasy"[19] were the ones that survived. While the Kingly and Ulster Cycles fell into disuse, "the Finn and Mythological Cycles flourished—or became decadent, if you like— accumulating folklore and magical motifs to the point where they grew first unintentionally and then deliberately ludicrous."[20] Joyce, then, was not an instigator when he wrote the "Cyclops" chapter of *Ulysses* in a wildly exaggerated style; and O'Brien's depiction of Finn can be seen not as a parody of Joyce's presentation but, in a wider context, as part of a tradition.

In the first extract, *"from my typescript descriptive of Finn MacCool and his people, being humorous or quasi-humorous incursion into ancient mythology"* (13), O'Brien is careful to establish a sense of ritual and formula appropriate to his material. Conan's request for Finn to tell particular stories—the Bull of Cooley, the feast of Bricriu, and so on—reminds us that the Finn Cycle was an oral, not a literary, tradition. The ritual of members of Finn's company, the Fianna, asking for particular tales is itself appropriate to the tradition. In earlier manuscript drafts of *At Swim* Finn occasionally lapsed into a deliberately deplorable modern idiom, but O'Brien changed this aspect during revision. And though Finn appears in the company of Shanahan, Furriskey, and Lamont, he never speaks out of his own legendary character, or directly to the others.

In the *"Synopsis, being a summary of what has gone before, FOR THE BENEFIT OF NEW READERS"* (60), the narrator explains that Finn has been hired by Trellis for his novel in order to protect Peggy, a servant girl who is also a character in his novel. (Peggy later marries Furriskey against Trellis's wishes while he is asleep.) The twentieth-century characters are kindly and dismissive, impressed and diffident about Finn's status as a storyteller: Shanahan says, "Five minutes ago he was giving out a yarn the length of my arm. . . . Right enough he is a terrible man for talk. Aren't you now? . . .'For a man of his years,' said Lamont, slowly and authoritatively, he can do the talking" (63).

Finn, however, seems oblivious to their presence, as though O'Brien decided to take chronology seriously: that is, the twentieth-century characters are able to hear and read tales of Finn, but not the other way around. Not only does Finn appear to be unaware of Furriskey and company; he needs Conan—in this case "hidden"—before he can perform: "Relate, said hidden Conan, the tale of the Feasting of Dún na nGedh." Finn's discourse and Shanahan's conversation are carried on simultaneously, very different, yet linked in subject matter. Lamont likes to hear a story "well told. I like to meet a man that can take in hand to tell a story and not make a balls of it while he's at it. I like to know where I am. . . . Everything has a beginning and an end" (63).

Furriskey, Shanahan, and Lamont ignore Conan's request and Finn's response, until Finn proclaims authoritatively, "I will relate," in answer to Conan's desire to hear the tale of Sweeny. ("The Frenzy of Sweeny," incidentally, was one of the poems O'Brien quoted in his M.A. thesis on Irish nature poetry at University College.) "We're off again,' said Furriskey. . . . Draw in your chairs, boys, said Shanahan, we're right for the night. We're away on a hack" (64). Their word choice is hardly appropriate to the heroic figure and his tale. Lamont is slightly more formal, but even so sounds incongruous: "Pray proceed, Sir."

After Conan's interjection "good for the telling," Finn is allowed several uninterrupted pages in which to develop his story. Sweeny's story prepares us for his later appearance as a character in the book. If we did not know the legend before, Shanahan considerately offers a summary:

* * *

The story, said learned Shanahan in a learned explanatory manner, is about
this fellow Sweeny that argued the toss with the clergy and came off second-best
at the wind-up. There was a curse—a malediction—put down in the book
against him. The upshot is your man became a bloody bird.
   I see, said Lamont.
   Do you see it, Mr. Furriskey, said Shanahan. What happens? He is
changed into a bird for his pains and he could go from here to Carlow in one hop.
Do you see it, Mr. Lamont? (85)

   The repetition of "learned," together with Shanahan's language and
hectoring manner, suggests that he is anything but learned; nevertheless
he has clearly been attentive, and offers another version of the story,
however vulgarized.
   When Finn includes Sweeny's song in his narrative (72), Shanahan
interrupts because he has been reminded of something: Finn's words
bring "the thing into my head in a rush"; and again, "that thing you were
saying reminds me of something bloody good." But Finn remains
oblivious to lack of interest in his tale and continues: "On the morning
of the third day thereafter, said Finn, he was flogged until he bled
water." In a masterly and seemingly impartial speech, Shanahan
proposes that although Finn's tale is "good stuff, bloody nice," it remains
above and beyond the understanding of common people: "But the man in
the street, where does he come in? By God he doesn't come in at all as far
as I can see." This question is crucial, one that O'Brien himself poses by
the act of writing *At Swim*—a comic critique of modernist novels that
have little interest for or in the common reader. But as the question is
raised by a character who is very much a man in the street himself, it lacks
authority and force. Shanahan upholds ancient legend—"You can't beat
it . . . the real old stuff of the native land, you know, stuff that brought
scholars to our shore when your men on the other side were flat on their
bellies before the calf of gold"—and denigrates it—"Feed yourself up on
that tack once and you won't want more for a long time." The argument
is complicated by national pride: "It's the stuff that put our country
where she stands today," a remark that can certainly be read ironically.
   Paradoxically, O'Brien presents a point of view that he holds himself,
in a context in which it can only be interpreted as antiintellectual and even
philistine. Shanahan feels superior to those who are unable to follow
Finn's tale; his comment "[I]t's not every man could see it, I'm bloody
sure of that, one in a thousand" is patronizing as well as characteristically
belligerent.

The fact that the three Dubliners' discussion concerns myth and legend is significant. Myth has a prominent place in modernist literature, its uses very different in the work of Joyce, Yeats, and Eliot from, for example, Renaissance or Victorian classical reference and allusion. Modernist writers appropriated myth with the dual purpose of (a) putting the modern individual—that is, the alienated and deracinated reader!—back in touch with his or her roots and unconscious and (b) providing a framework for their own poems or narratives. O'Brien mocks this kind of use when he has Finn proclaim:

> I am an Ulsterman, a Connachtman, a Greek, said Finn.
> I am Cuchulain, I am Patrick.
> I am Carbery-Cathead, I am Goll.
> I am my own father and my own son.
> I am every hero from the crack of time. (19)

Apart from any literary critical questions raised by Shanahan's objection to Finn's poem, it serves the purpose of introducing a modern—and degenerate—equivalent in the form of Jem Casey's poem "Workman's Friend." Shanahan, eager to impress his audience, attempts to dignify his recitation in terms similar to those he has used about "the real old stuff": "[T]he name or title of the pome I am about to recite, gentlemen, said Shanahan, with leisure priest-like in character, is a pome by the name of the "Workman's Friend." " He cites testimonials and indicates its general application:

> I've heard it praised by the highest. It's a pome about a thing that's known to all of us. It's about a drink of porter.
> When things go wrong and will not come right,
> Though you do the best you can,
> When life looks black as the hour of the night
> A PINT OF PLAIN IS YOUR ONLY MAN.

Like Sweeny, Jem Casey appears later in the book, though unlike Sweeny he is a fictional creation of O'Brien's. Finn dozes during the recital of "Workman's Friend" but resumes his story where he left off, until Shanahan is obliged to interrupt again, this time with a verse of his own that shows the influence of Finn's poem and Jem Casey's: "Listen man. Listen to this before it's lost. When stags appear on the mountain high, with flanks the colour of bran, when a badger bold can say good-bye, A PINT OF PLAIN IS YOUR ONLY MAN!" (80). The form of the verse

is Casey's but Finn's influence is strong; at the point Shanahan interrupts,
Finn has just mentioned badgers and stags—and "bran," though used
here as an adjective, was actually the name of Finn's dog in legend.

Lamont affirms that the "Workman's Friend" will "live," and asks
Finn's opinion: "Give the company the benefit of your scholarly
pertinacious fastidious opinion, Sir Storybook." Consistently enough,
Finn fails to engage with him, continuing instead with his story against a
background of Shanahan's and Lamont's desultory platitudes. Furriskey's
remark "Let him talk . . . it'll do him good. It has to come out
somewhere" (78) can be read in two ways: storytelling may be regarded as
some kind of therapy for Finn (which would link the use of myth here
with one of its psychological functions in modernist writing), or else it
implies effluent, some kind of waste product that is better out than
in—diametrically opposed views of the value of Finn's story, both
characteristically irrelevant. It is typical that O'Brien's characters are
critical of one another's creations; criticism and countercriticism occur
throughout the novel, allowing primacy to no one genre or style, not the
hero-tale, or the poet-of-the-people's verse, or the narrator's manuscript
that contains them all—or his biographical frame-tale.

Another group of Trellis's characters set out for the Red Swan
Hotel—where Trellis and the others live—in order to do battle for the
soul of a child that is about to be born. The Pooka MacPhellimey—"a
member of the devil class"—is visited by the Good Fairy, who tells him
that Sheila Lamont is about to give birth: "The child is expected, said
the Good Fairy, tomorrow evening. I shall be there and shall endeavour
to put the child under my benevolent influence for life. To go there alone,
however, without informing you of the happy event, that would be a
deplorable breach of etiquette. Let the pair of us go therefore, and let the
best man of us win the day" (111). The extended colloquies between the
Pooka and the Good Fairy (who was originally called an Angel in the
manuscript) are one of the major delights of At Swim. Although the
Pooka is classified as a kind of devil, he is courteous and harmless; the
Good Fairy, on the other hand, smokes cigarettes and is frequently tetchy
and bad tempered.

The journey to the Red Swan is a parody of medieval romance, the
hard travail through rough terrain in search of truth. T. S. Eliot's poem
The Waste Land takes this form, a quest for spirituality through desolate
London streets, with little certainty that anything has been found at the
end. Ulysses is a similar quest narrative, though without religious

overtones in a conventional sense. The simplest example of a modern romance, however, is the film *Star Wars,* in which there is little ambiguity. Good triumphs over evil, and innumerable difficulties are confronted and surmounted, not only by quick wits but by faith in the face of adversity.

O'Brien's characters have none of these qualities. They wander aimlessly, bickering about the quality of the material of the Pooka's coat:

Some of these trees are sharp, [the Good Fairy] observed, mind or you will make a tatters of your coat.

There is better stuff in that coat, said the Pooka with a wilful march on a wall of thornsticks, than they are putting into clothes nowadays. A coat in the old days was made to stand up to rough wear and was built to last.

Keep to the left, called the Good Fairy. Do you always carry on like this when you are walking?

I do not mind telling you, said the Pooka courteously, that there is no subterfuge of economy more misconceived than the purchase of cheap factory-machined clothing. (114)

The desultory conversation is sustained until they meet and are joined by Slug Willard and Shorty Andrews, the incongruous cowboys whom Trellis filched from Mr. Tracey's novels to serve his own. Like the Wise Men traveling to Bethlehem, they are aware that it is customary to take gifts, and while searching in the undergrowth for "blood-gutted berries and wrinkled cresses, branches of juice-slimed sloes, whortles and plums . . . the speckled eggs from the nests of daws" they find "Jem by God Casey," poet of the people, in a clump of bushes. The style that introduces him is the same as that which introduces Sweeny, whom they find in a similar situation a little later on their journey: "There was a prolonged snapping of stiffened rods and stubborn shoots and the sharp agony of fractured branches, the pitiless flogging against each other of green life-laden leaves, the thrashing and the scourging of a clump in torment" (118). The pain and suffering that are implied are totally inappropriate for the figure in cloth cap and muffler who emerges unscathed—Jem Casey has been in the bush "reciting a pome to a selection of [his] friends," not relieving himself as Slug and Shorty prefer to imagine. Sweeny, by contrast, is in a bad way: "He came to the ground with his right nipple opened to the wide and a ruined back that was packed with thorns" (126). His "tormented cress-stained mouth never halting from the recital of inaudible strange staves" very different from Jem Casey's verses "The Gift of God is a Working Man."

Sweeny takes up his story, reciting stanzas from his own "Frenzy," from which Finn recited earlier for Shanahan and Lamont. Like Finn, Sweeny does not engage with the modern characters, though they concern themselves with his well-being: Shorty the cowboy is anxious to put a bullet through him to put him out of his pain; the Good Fairy recommends gin and a bottle of beer; and Casey, recognizing a fellow poet, does what he can by packing Sweeny's wounds with green moss. Sweeny is taken along with them but continues to inhabit his own isolated world of madness and misery.

Conclusion

O'Brien asked John Garvin, a colleague in the civil service, for a Greek epigraph for *At Swim-Two-Birds*. Garvin supplied one that was taken from Euripides's *Hercules Furens* "in consideration of the corresponding agony of Sweeny."[21] The title of the novel might suggest that Sweeny is in fact the center of the work, for it does occur once in the text: Sweeny "set forth in the air again till he reached the church at Snámh-dá-én (or Swim-Two-Birds" [68]). But this view would be misleading, particularly as O'Brien left final decisions about the title to his publishers. He suggested "The Next Market Day," "Sweet-Scented Manuscript," "Truth Is an Odd Number," "Task-Master's Eye," "Through an Angel's Eye-lid," and "Sweeny in the Trees." His own opinion was that "Sweeny in the Trees" was "preferable to At Swim-Two-Birds," which he liked less and less,"[22] but his agent wrote to say, "The title *At Swim-Two-Birds* is so difficult that I have got rather attached to it, and perhaps Longmans feel the same way."[23]

Garvin chose the epigraph with care. His own translation from the Greek reads, "For all things go out and give place one to another," in recognition, as he said, of the "rapid succession of characters and plots right through the novel."[24] Nothing could be more appropriate, particularly as no translation is offered. Average readers are not necessarily classical scholars, and the epigraph that gives a clue to the bewildering succession of narratives that make up the book is thus as obscure as they are.

How should we read *At Swim?* The narrative keeps us at a distance. Its fragmentary construction dictates our response, and we are never in danger of experiencing "a real concern for the fortunes of illusory characters," as the narrator puts it (25). This construction prohibits "conventional" responses, and the inclusion of extracts and quotations from literature of all sorts actually forces us to admit and accept the element of chance incorporated into the novel. When Longman's accepted it, O'Brien indulged himself in self-parody concerning its structure:

It is disturbing to think that there is so much irresponsibility in the London publishing business. I certainly had no idea that the book in its present form would be touched by anyone. I have just glanced at it for the first time and there can be no doubt that parts of it are terrible. Owing to its admirable analytical construction, however, the diseased bits can easily be cut out and replaced—possibly by a few pages of the Berlin Telephone Directory of which I have a copy, 1919 edition. I will refrain from surgical work till I hear from you, however.[25]

Once *At Swim* was published, he seems to have thought of it in much the same way he thought of the works of those writers whose books he himself had used: they exist and as such are fair game, there to be plundered by succeeding generations. He disliked the book but was deeply impressed by Henri Morisset's French translation: "Your masterly translation tempts me to think it is not as bad as I thought." The qualities O'Brien praises are not necessarily those one might expect: "I found your resource, improvisation, unshakeable nerve and occasional audacity very impressive indeed."[26] Later in the same year he wrote: "As you know this AS2B gives me a pain in the neck, even if I've never read it, but I found KERMESSE[27] diverting, eerie, occasionally quite funny. The translator shows great enterprise and iron nerves."[28] The German translation of *At Swim, Zwei Vögel beim Schwimmen,* did not elicit quite the same unstinting admiration, but O'Brien wrote, "By the insanity that informs all publishing, this *ZVbS* might actually sell widely. . . . I am much taken with 'der Pooka MacPhellimey.' "[29]

One venture he fondly envisaged—but that was never carried out—depended for its success on finding someone to translate *Kermesse* back into English: "MacGibbon and Kee then publish in paperback a tripartite volume which will contain in this order (i) AS2B: (ii) KERMESSE IRLANDAISE: (iii) the new book."[30] The point of the exercise, like the game of Chinese whispers, would be to see just how much the last differed from the first. Nothing could demonstrate more effectively O'Brien's delight in randomness. While he was frequently outraged by critics or reviewers of his fiction, no creative comment in the form of work based on his own ever seems to have received his strictures. He was, for example, delighted with Hugh Leonard's adaptation of *The Dalkey Archive* for the stage.

O'Brien was concerned to exercise control over his reader but not over the uses particular readers might make of his text. He wants us to be surprised and baffled; he wants to frustrate accustomed responses—but he seems happy to allow total freedom in the forming of any kind of oblique, anarchic, or creative response. *At Swim* has some things in common with Sterne's extraordinary *Life and Opinions of Tristram Shandy;*[31] in many ways it, like Sterne's work, is an *anti*novel. We are not treated as if we were "dear readers," or gentle, kind, or honored ones—O'Brien, like Sterne, sends up such conventions. Instead we are allowed to be sharp or simple—anything but overreverent or pretentious. O'Brien knew that some readers would make a labor of the book, and there is certainly plenty of matter to occupy us should we choose to read *At Swim* in this way. But O'Brien's describing it to Ethel Mannin as a "belly laugh" or "high-class literary pretentious slush" was acute as much as it was self-depreciatory, for it implies numerous positions for readers to adopt between those two poles, and few novelists give their readers such license.

Chapter Three
The Third Policeman

Narrative Strategies and the Plot

O'Brien's second novel, *The Third Policeman,*[1] is a work of grim black comedy. He tried unsuccessfully to have it published in the months following its completion, and invented stories about the loss of the manuscript rather than admit it had been rejected. In fact he filed it safely away until the early 1960s, when he began to rework the material into *The Dalkey Archive.* *The Third Policeman* itself was not published until 1967, after O'Brien's death in 1966.

The earliest surviving reference to what was to become *The Third Policeman* comes in a letter from O'Brien to Andy Gillett. "I have not yet done anything about another novel beyond turning over some ideas in my head," he wrote, but the second paragraph of this letter shows that the "ideas" were fairly well advanced: "Briefly, the story I have in mind opens as a very orthodox murder mystery in a rural district. The perplexed parties have recourse to the local barrack which, however, contains some very extraordinary policemen who do not confine their investigations or activities to this world or to any known planes or dimensions. Their most casual remarks create a thousand other mysteries but there will be no question of the difficulties of the last book. The whole point of my plan will be the most brain-staggering imponderables of the policemen."[2]

It was not until January of the following year, 1940, that he mentioned what is really the most fascinating aspect of the work: "I think the plot is quite new and nowadays that alone is something to be slightly proud of." The plot of the novel is intimately bound up with the policeman's activities, but the main interest centers on narrative strategies that O'Brien resorted to in order to keep the surprise denouement from his reader, a remarkable technical achievement as the fiction has the form of a first-person narrative, and yet the unnamed protagonist remains as bewildered by the unfolding events as his reader does.

The Third Policeman has been described as a circular novel. This description is not quite accurate, for although the end of the book certainly takes us back, it does not return us to the novel's opening, as Joyce's *Finnegans Wake* does. *The Third Policeman* begins with a somewhat shocking statement: "Not everybody knows how I killed old Philip Mathers, smashing his jaw in with my spade." The narrator then describes his childhood, the deaths of his parents, and the circumstances that led to his association with John Divney, his partner in crime. Motivation for the murder is robbery: on Divney's part, purely for personal gain, and on the narrator's because he believes his mission in life is to publish the "De Selby Index," an academic work that preoccupies him to the exclusion of all that can be regarded as normal life. On the night of the murder, Divney hides Mathers's cashbox, concealing its whereabouts from the narrator. Three years later the men return to the scene of the crime to retrieve it, and it is at this point in the novel that the narrative complications really begin: reader and narrator alike are unaware that Divney murders the narrator.

O'Brien manages this point with skill, distracting our attention at this crucial moment so that while the world of the text certainly becomes extraordinary, it still conforms to a curious logic. William Golding's *Pincher Martin* and Ambrose Bierce's short story "An Occurrence at Owl Creek Bridge" also make use of dead or dying narrators, and like those fictions, *The Third Policeman* presents a very particular case of advance retrospection when we come to reread it. The text conceals all that is clearly revealed in subsequent readings. For example, the following extract does not have the same significance initially as it does on later reading; the event we might expect to be drawn to our attention is not emphasized in a conventional way:

Just when my hand should be closing about the box something happened.

I cannot hope to describe it but it frightened me very much before I had understood it even slightly. It was some change which came upon me or upon the room, indescribably subtle, yet momentous, ineffable. . . . My senses were bewildered all at once and could give no explanation. The fingers of my right hand . . . had found nothing at all. . . . The box was gone! (20–21)

This is the point at which the narrator describes his own death. But because the experience is as unfamiliar for the reader as it is for the narrator, and because the action that was begun before "the change" took place is completed afterward, the reader is encouraged to ignore the more mystical something-happened-but-I-don't-know-what writing in favor of the concrete detail,—"The box was gone!"—which within the context of the story is sensational and more easily understood. The exclamation point draws attention to this event as the important one, and the fact that "The box was gone!" is placed at the end of a paragraph, imitating the end of the previous paragraph, wherein the search for the box began, helps to distract attention from the real crux of the episode: the narrator's death, which occurs between the two. We notice little change in his control of his descriptions from this point—though this aspect must be partly attributed to the "odd" nature of the preceding narrative realism (which will be examined later).

The narrator continues to exist and, in his ignorance, contemplates death on several occasions. This strengthens the reader's conviction that he is in fact alive. His response to the death sentence pronounced by Inspector O'Corky is nothing if not vital: "I will resist," he shouts, "and will resist to the death and fight for my existence even if I lose my life in the attempt" (85). The notion of "I'll live if it kills me" is comic, and the narrator's seriousness is doubtless intended to be funny, but when we reread the book, the humor is colored with pathos because we know, whereas he does not, that he is already dead. Lack of awareness is a major source of comedy (whether the character involved is fictional or actual); however, comedy of this kind is usually a double-edged sword: the husband unaware of the lipstick on his collar looks foolish, but from his wife's point of view the sight is not guaranteed to provoke laughter.

The narrator's ignorance of his own death has a slightly different effect in the following instance: "Down into the earth where dead men go I would go soon and maybe come out of it again in some healthy way, free and innocent of all human perplexity" (137). Here we are invited to sympathize with the narrator's longing to be free from the complexity of existence, perhaps even to share his feelings. The implications for this sympathy are chilling, for when we reread, we are sharply aware that, as far as this novel is concerned, freedom, innocence, and understanding are forever beyond human reach. The narrator has actually become immortal, but he is unaware of the fact and will never be in a position to understand, because he is beyond redemption. Such consequences account for the "blackness" of O'Brien's comedy.

Common sense suggests that fear of dying belongs only to the living, and so the reader never thinks about the possibility that the narrator is dead. Use of tactile physical images also encourages us to fail to question his state. We are more likely to associate qualities of *not* feeling with death—"Soon my brain would be changed to wood completely and I would then be dead" (100)—whereas the narrator, isolated and miserable, describes the familiar sensation of the lump in the throat: "I felt my brain cluttered and stuffed with questions and blind perplexity and I also felt the sadness of my position coming back into my throat" (97). A "large emotion came swelling against my throat and filling my mind with great sorrow" (121), he says, and in the lift on the way to eternity he "felt his stomach bounding sickeningly about inside . . . as if it were a wet football filled with water" (112). Traditionally, insubstantiality is connected with death, and that assumption, too, prevents us from questioning the narrator's existence.

While we may feel inclined to reread *Pincher Martin* and "Occurrence at Owl Creek Bridge" immediately to see how we could have been misled, O'Brien does not leave such matters to chance: the last two pages of *The Third Policeman* reproduce almost exactly an incident occurring earlier so that the reader is also obliged to repeat his experience. Rounding a bend in the road, the narrator says, "An extraordinary spectacle was presented to me. About a hundred yards away was a house which astonished me. It looked as if it were painted like an advertisement on a board on the roadside and, indeed, very poorly painted" (47, 171). The narrative returns not to the opening of the novel or yet to the scene of the murder but to a point after the protagonist had left the "murdered" man and after his encounter with Martin Finnucane, the captain of the one-legged men. The repeated passage deals with the protagonist's first sight of the police barrack up to his meeting with the first of the policemen. In its second appearance the passage is slightly shorter; nine sentences—mainly descriptive—have been cut, and a new passage, dealing with John Divney's arrival, is added. Nonetheless, such key phrases as "I had never seen with my eyes ever in my life before anything so unnatural and appalling" (46, 171) are repeated—enough of them to recall the earlier passage and to convey the horror of repetition to the reader.

There is a certain fascination in precisely repeating any sequence of events; recurring dreams (even if not nightmares) have a horrid fascination simply because they recur, and a feeling of déjà vu is always unsettling. And when O'Brien implies that the events of his novel are endlessly doomed to repeat, and his protagonist must go through the business of trying to understand his surroundings, lose that understanding, and begin again and again, the writer is appealing to what may be an unconscious horror in us all. There is a clear distinction between the comfortable, repetitive, remembered patterns on which we build our lives and the unbidden system that threatens to take us over. The implications are sinister not only for the protagonist but also for the reader, who is doomed to enact the same movement, as the narrative repeats itself. A curious illusion is created, for when we reread *any* novel, we embark on a hauntingly familiar journey of complication and crisis with the hero, who always, as we read, has to undergo the process of education once more. But "conventional" novels rarely leave their protagonist in exactly the same situation as he or she was at the outset. The main character is usually older and wiser, if nothing else, and these are precisely what O'Brien's protagonist is not.

The reader of *The Third Policeman* has access to recollection as he or she rereads the book, but the narrator has no memory and thus cannot learn from experience. Having told his story, he, unlike his reader, has no access to the pages he has written. In fact, it is important that O'Brien reproduces those earlier pages at the end of his book, for there *is* a difference between the protagonist's experience and the reader's retrospective reading: on his second "journey" the narrator is accompanied by John Divney, though his presence will be no comfort. The world of the policemen will be equally bewildering, but a moral element is introduced: Divney too is being punished, for the murder of his companion, the narrator.

The Third Policeman may not be a straightforwardly "cyclical" novel; it is, as we have seen, more complicated than that. But inevitably its circular nature focuses our attention on the text itself as we reread, in a way that more conventional novels do not necessarily do. The way in which it was written is brought to our attention, emphasized, as we try to discover the part we played in aiding and abetting the delusion worked on us.

An interesting question arises from the form of *The Third Policeman* as a direct result of it being a first-person narrative. Where and when, we may ask, is the story told? We sit at Dowell's fireside to "hear" Ford Madox Ford's *The Good Soldier,* a fellow sailor later recounts Marlow's story in Conrad's *The Heart of Darkness;* the narrator of *At Swim-Two-Birds* writes in his stuffy bedroom. From what position or perspective does the narrator of *The Third Policeman* tell his story? It is impossible to say: it is written in the past tense, but the narrator's memory is limited and seems to become more so. He can recall his childhood at the start of the novel, but this memory does not seem to play any part as he reembarks on events at the end. Yet he does have recollections of the "real" world throughout, and this fact is important, because otherwise the world he is condemned to inhabit would not be so frightening. Ultimately all that can be said is that there is no provision in the text for the "space" from which the story is recounted. In a letter to William Saroyan, O'Brien wrote, "When you are writing about the world of the dead—and the damned—where none of the rules and laws (not even the law of gravity) holds good, there is any amount of scope for back-chat and funny cracks."[3] He could well have concluded his sentence by saying that none of the rules and laws of fiction hold good either.

Narrative Contracts

Jonathon Culler describes the relationship between the reader and a novel as a "narrative contract." "The basic convention governing the novel," he writes, "is the expectation that readers will, through their contact with the text, be able to recognise a world which it produces or to which it refers."[4] The principle on which *The Third Policeman* is written is a violation of this expectation; the narrative contract between narrator and reader is established only to be violated. It is not simply a "trick" at the reader's expense, because the narrator too is unaware of the exact significance of what befalls him. Some of the oddities in the narrator's descriptions of his early life may, we see retrospectively, be accounted for because he is already dead and damned when he recalls it.

The opening paragraph is interesting from a structural point of view both with regard to the rest of the novel and in the relation it establishes between reader, narrator, and story. The novel might more conventionally have begun with the second paragraph, "I was born a long time ago," but instead it begins in medias res: violence is established at the outset, and in such a way that we expect the murder to be described more fully later. Our reading, then, is going to reenact the protagonist's experience when he recounts the events of the novel.

The second paragraph derives from the bildungsroman convention: a long tradition of novels that describe the hero's or heroine's life from birth or very early days to maturity (few novels follow the protagonist beyond the grave, though many leave him there). It is this derivation which emphasizes the uncertainties of the childhood episode in *The Third Policeman*—the reader is in unfamiliar territory. The sentence "I was born a long time ago" gives us a false clue; we may suppose this voice to be an old man's. The use of specific names, Parnell and Ireland, gives us a definite context and a point of historical reference in the real, objective, historical world we know: if it crosses our minds at all, we could be fairly confident that the text is giving us a representation of the world in which we live. But that expectation is undermined by incongruities that emerge.

For example, how literally should we take the statement that the narrator "never saw [his] mother out of the kitchen in [his] life"? One such odd statement might pass unnoticed, but the opening page is full of them. The pub is closed most of the day because "my mother was always in the kitchen," but not, it seems, because her duties demanded her presence there: "[S]he spent her life making tea to pass the time and singing snatches of song to pass the meantime."

The public house emerges as a strange place, and one feels as if whole elements of life—emotion, morals, and a good livelihood—are omitted, either because the narrator grew up without them or because he is now so far beyond that he cannot remember. Even at the outset there is something disquieting about this novel; it is not, as O'Brien described it, "a very orthodox murder mystery in a rural district." By its very nature, *The Third Policeman* requires an unstable narrative contract. From the beginning we are prompted to question our understanding of the world created by the text, but in the circumstances we are also likely to find an odd family life unsurprising—we expect that this oddity will have helped to produce a murderer. It is important to hold both views, because although the texture of the world of the novel changes after the moment of the narrator's death, this texture must not (from the author's point of view) be seen to change so drastically that the denouement is obvious at that point. Only after the narrator's death do impossible events occur, but because childhood and youth have been described in ambiguous and uncertain terms, the reader is the more easily deceived.

In *A Colder Eye* Hugh Kenner discusses the unusual qualities inherent in English language that has been "strained and stressed by Irish habits of thought."[5] English works "from verb to verb," whereas Irish depends much more on nouns, the effect being a series of static, vivid pictures rather than a sense of continuous action. Even this "highly aspective" verbal system fails to account, however, for the sentence construction at the beginning of *The Third Policeman,* which seems deliberately naive and enigmatic: "I never saw my mother outside the kitchen in my life and never saw a customer during the day [why would he, if the pub is only open at night?] and even at night I never saw more than two or three together." How literally are we intended to take the statement that his mother was always in the kitchen? The word *and* is used here very much as a child might use it, simply to join ideas together, but we may wonder whether there is a logical—indecent—association in the linking of mother and customers implied in the following: "But then I was in bed part of the time and it is possible that things happened differently with

my mother and the customers late at night." We cannot feel certain
whether we are being presented with a sociological case history to explain
our protagonist's subsequent disaffection and alienation or simply with a
description of a small-time, rather unsuccessful public house. "I knew her
well," the narrator says of his mother, "but my father and I were strangers
and did not converse much; often indeed when I would be studying in the
kitchen late at night I could hear him through the thin door to the shop
talking there from his seat under the oil lamps for hours on end to Mick
his sheep dog. . . .He was a man who understood all dogs thoroughly
and treated them like human beings." The father treats human beings by
ignoring his family's presence and talking to the dog. Either the father or
the narrator clearly has unusual attitudes. Our confidence is further
undermined, and our doubts raised about the ability of language to
describe the universe adequately. Language is still seen as imprecise if we
decide that the author's intention was comic, for "the world" being
described is so imperfectly realized at this early stage that we have no
point of reference from which to confidently perceive comic social
deviance.

The Third Policeman is, in fact, a fantasy—but a "disguised" one.
Instead of declaring itself to be fantastic, the world created by the text
bears just enough resemblance to a straightforward, recognizable one of
the realist tradition to be disturbing in its differences. O'Brien's treatment
of landscape is masterly in this respect:

The road was narrow, white, old, hard and scarred with shadow. It ran away
westwards in the mist of the early morning, running cunningly through the little
hills and going to some trouble to visit tiny towns which were not, strictly
speaking, on its way. It was possibly one of the oldest roads in the world. I found
it hard to think of a time when there was no road there because the trees and the
tall hills and the fine views of the bog-land had been arranged by wise hands for
the pleasing picture they made when looked at from the road. Without a road to
have them looked at from they would have a somewhat aimless if not futile
aspect. (33)

The narrator's thought processes here, of course, have been shaped by his
mentor, de Selby, whose ideas about the universe are not strictly
conventional. But the sentence structure is awkward, deliberately drawing
attention to itself. "Without a road to have them looked at from"
emphasizes the ambiguity of thought expressed and suggests that the
whole world is created for the sake of subjective human response—as the
hell the narrator inhabits must be.

O'Brien's narrator becomes aware of the strangeness of the landscape: "Everything seemed almost too pleasant, too perfect, too finely made. . . . Trees were arranged here and there with far-from-usual consideration for the fastidious eye'' (35). That the narrator perceives design at work in his surroundings implies that he—like Golding's Pincher Martin—has created it himself or that it has been specially created for him; even so, the world he inhabits is not as familiar as he would like it to be. O'Brien writes as if he is commenting on the fact that he is describing an invented world, and this artificial, stage-flat effect is inevitable if a writer will insist on creating anew. It is as if there is an implicit reference, and a direct contrast, to the views of the narrator in *At Swim-Two-Birds: he* felt that a writer should create only when no preexisting fiction would serve. The first view of the police barrack supports this "self-conscious" reading: "It was momentous and frightening; the whole morning and the whole world seemed to have no purpose at all save to frame it and give it some magnitude and position so that I could find it with my simple senses and pretend to myself that I understood it" (47).

The novelist's purpose is almost precisely identical: to create a plausible setting for the barrack and an environment for his character to operate in. All fictional landscapes are anything but "real"; they simply exist for the sake of the fiction. If a character walks along a road, a road is supplied—if not specifically by the novelist's description, then by the reader's imagination, triggered by the simple use of the word *road.* Each reader's mental picture will be different, but with generally fair accuracy to other parts of the text. Though O'Brien claimed that in this novel there would be none of the "fireworks" of *At Swim-Two-Birds,* in descriptions like this one we can see that the self-consciousness and self-reflexivity of the earlier work continued to absorb him.

The Importance of Names

Like the first-person narrator of *At Swim,* the protagonist of *The Third Policeman* has no name, a technical feat that deliberately makes discussion of the central character somewhat awkward. In *At Swim* O'Brien's aim was partly a jest directed at the modernist orthodoxy of authorial absence. In *The Third Policeman* the namelessness has a slightly different, though equally appropriate function. "Not naming" helps to prevent overly simple reader sympathy: it is less easy to identify with someone who remains nameless. O'Brien was always aware of, and concerned to

undermine, the common assumption that when we read fiction we engage
in an equivalent of "lived experience." Such an assumption would be a
supreme joke given that the narrator of *The Third Policeman* is dead. But
even more important for this particular novel, the narrator cannot
remember his own name, a lapse that becomes increasingly vital (and
unfortunate) during the course of the book.

Difficult though the first chapter is in terms of conventional realism,
the fantasy takes off in the second, three years after Mathers has been
murdered, when the narrator and John Divney return to the scene of the
crime to retrieve the black box.

"Remember this," [Divney instructs the narrator]. "If you meet anybody, you
don't know what you're looking for, you don't know in whose house you are, you
don't know anything."

"I don't even know my own name," I answered. This was a very remarkable
thing for me to say because the next time I was asked my name I could not
answer. I did not know. (18).

The episode dealing with the narrator's death has been discussed
earlier in this chapter; after that episode the narrator, still in Mathers's
house, encounters and recognizes his own victim, who appears to be alive.
Overcoming his horror, the narrator eventually speaks to Mathers, but
conversation is difficult because to each of the narrator's questions
Mathers replies in the negative: " 'Are you dead at present?' I asked. 'I am
not' " (23). And again, "Do you know where the box is?" "No" (24).
Eventually, the narrator mistakenly feels a sense of achievement when,
couching a question in a double negative, he elicits the same answer as
usual, but with positive results: " 'Will you refuse to answer a straight
question?' I asked. 'I will not,' he replied" (25).

Pleased, the narrator mistakenly feels that he has mastered the
situation: "It meant that my mind had got to grips with his, that I was
now almost arguing with him and that we were behaving like ordinary
human beings." Conversation of a kind is established, the narrator gains a
mistaken illusion of normality, and he pursues his original aim: to
discover the location of the black box. It is at this point that Mathers
breaks the sequence, responding to the insistent "Where is it?" with a
question of his own: " 'What is your name?' he asked sharply" (27).
Shocked, the narrator realizes that he cannot answer: "I did not know my
name, did not remember who I was. I was not certain where I had come

from. . . . I was sure of nothing save my search for the black box. . . . I had no name. 'I have no name,' I replied" (27).

Loss of memory is a terrifying prospect; if one's personal history is lost, then there is nothing on which to base the construct of identity or individuality, nothing to account for the self that is summed up and signified by one's name. O'Brien recognizes this idea but typically turns the narrator's crisis into one of grotesque comedy. In reply to "I have no name," Mathers says that in that case it would be impossible for him to surrender the black box, as the narrator would be unable to sign a receipt. "That would be most irregular," Mathers says. "I might as well give it to the west wind or to the smoke from a pipe' "—in other words, to something ephemeral, without substance: precisely like the dead narrator, were he aware of the fact.

At first, it seems as if O'Brien is unwilling or unable to sustain or confront the serious implications raised by the narrator's loss of self. Mathers's logic—signing a receipt—seems a wildly inappropriate response, but this kind of comedy is repeated with increasingly dark connotations throughout the novel. In chapter 7, for example, the narrator, who by now has been condemned to death, tries to use "logic" in a similar way to his own advantage. He reminds the policeman that he told him that "I was not here at all because I had no name and that my personality was invisible to the law." The policeman agrees that this was so, and the narrator counters with a very astute question: "Then how can I be hanged for a murder?" (86). The policeman asks whether he is absolutely sure that this is the case and suggests 29 possible names, all of which the narrator rejects. The problem is resolved, however, when the policeman argues that as he is nameless—"a piece of negative nullility neutralized"—then "[f]or that reason alone . . . we can take you and hang the life out of you and there is no entry to be made in the death papers" (88). Seemingly logical, ludicrously comic, totally absurd, and callous, but in fact potentially very serious indeed if we think of a parallel in the world we inhabit: the way in which political prisoners can become "non persons" and disappear.

Having no name is equated with loss of identity in the novel. In the third chapter, the narrator seems not deeply perturbed but dwells on how "tantalizing" it is to have forgotten his name: "All people have names of one kind or another. Some are arbitrary labels related to the appearance of the person, some represent purely genealogical associations but most afford some clue as to parents of the person named and confer a certain advantage in the execution of legal documents. Even a dog has a name which distinguishes him from other dogs" (36). By implication, the narrator's status is lower than that of a dog, and he has no recollection of his origins.

It is from a blend of pure fantasy with remorseless *seeming* logic that *The Third Policeman* derives its grotesque comedy. The propositions about the physical laws that govern the world in which the narrator finds himself seem to make scientific sense but are in fact absurd. His failure to recognize that he has passed from one world to another accounts for the uneasiness. The book would be merely funny were it not for the fact that the narrator, time and time again, believes he has grasped principles on which those around him operate; again, however, blurring of distinctions between the world before death and that after death makes understanding impossible. In the first chapter, Divney, when questioned about the whereabouts of the black box, parried in much the same way as the murdered Mathers does: "I asked him where the box was a hundred times in a thousand different ways. He never answered in the same way but the answer was always the same. It was in a safe place" (16). Countless words, endless variations of language—to no purpose. As Mathers says, explaining his rule of always answering "no": "The system leads to peace and contentment. . . . People do not trouble to ask you questions if they know the answer is a foregone conclusion" (27). The use of double negatives, however, does allow Mathers to accept whiskey from friends, a comic example of human frailty operating in the world of the dead! If life can be manipulated by use of language, so can death, as these two examples show. The narrator's hell consists not of the traditional notion of the unrelieved physical pain of everlasting fires but of his torment in being deprived of the crucial knowledge that he is being punished.

According to traditional beliefs, we have souls that leave our bodies at the moment of death. O'Brien uses this idea to confuse his reader, for the narrator has a soul with whom he converses, and thus cannot be dead yet. Again, we are not being convinced that the narrator is alive but, rather, being prevented from questioning it.

O'Brien was not happy with this aspect of his novel, he wrote to Pat Duggan, a publisher to whom he had sent the manuscript: "I intended to kill completely a certain repulsive and obtrusive character called Joe."[6] Joe's role in the novel is really simply a device to allow the narrator to commune with an inner self; Joe's knowledge is as limited as his own. Occasionally Joe functions as a kind of conscience, reminding the narrator, for example, that the American gold watch he claims to have lost (a fiction he has begun to accept as a fact) never existed (46). Sometimes he is simply an excuse for the kind of comic irrelevance O'Brien enjoys indulging in: when the narrator is asked his name, or when in the third chapter he suggests various names to himself—Hugh Murray, Constantin Petrie, Peter Small, Dr. Solway Garr, and so on—Joe, equally arbitrarily, suggests Signor Beniamino Bari, "the eminent tenor" (36). He follows this suggestion with an imaginative re-creation of scenes outside La Scala—a scenario ludicrously remote from the countryside through which the narrator is walking and which has no connection with him.

Joe's contributions are always presented in italics, setting his words apart from those of the other characters in the novel and reminding the reader of his incorporeal status: again distracting us from questioning the narrator's existence. On the night before the execution is due to take place, Joe and the narrator discuss what happens after death: *"You have no idea where you are going . . . when all this is over?"* "No, none." *"Nor have I. I do not know, or do not remember, what happens to the like of me in these circumstances. Sometimes I think that perhaps I might become part of . . . the world, if you understand me?"* "I know" (140). Joe's speech undoubtedly becomes sentimental as he imagines becoming a part of nature—perhaps it is this quality that led O'Brien to call him "repulsive." The important point, though, is that Joe's knowledge is as limited as the narrator's, and he is equally doomed, for death has failed to release him from the body and character of his host.

Logic and Illogic

The Third Policeman gains most of its effectiveness, as we have seen, from the narrator's (and inevitably the reader's) limited knowledge but optimistic belief that he will eventually understand what is happening to him—a benefit that is finally conferred on the reader, but not on the main character. Elements in the text deliberately encourage narrator and reader alike to believe that the surroundings are familiar, and yet ultimately fail to yield that very familiarity which we expect. Nowhere is this more obvious than in the figures of the policemen. They are country policemen, solid, reassuring, slow, and methodical: we expect down-to-earth practicalities from them. O'Brien, needless to say, turns all these expectations on their head; the policemen may at first appear to be solid and unimaginative, yet they are figures of absolute fantasy. Policeman

MacCruiskeen occupies his off-duty hours making identical boxes that
nest inside one another, the largest of which alone prompts the narrator's
awe-filled and solemn respect, so delicate is the workmanship: "It is
nearly too nice," he says, "to talk about it . . . It is unmentionable" (61).
MacCruiskeen spent two years of his youth making the box, deciding
then that only an identical box would be content worthy enough for it.
The narrator's composure is severely shaken by its perfection, but he
becomes truly afraid when the total number of boxes-inside-boxes
arranged on the table before him amount to 29:

What he was doing was no longer wonderful but terrible. I shut my eyes and
prayed that he would stop while doing things that were at least possible for a man
to do. When I looked again I was happy that there was nothing to see and that he
had put no more of the chests prominently on the table but he was working to
the left with the invisible thing in his hand. . . .When he felt my look he came
over to me and gave me an enormous magnifying-glass. . . .I felt the muscles
around my heart tightening painfully as I took the instrument. (64).

Again, his fear is expressed in terms of physical symptoms, and he
comments on the strain such work must be on MacCruiskeen's eyes:
"determined to pretend that everybody was an ordinary person like
myself" (65). But his offhand verbal response does not conceal the fact
that he has been truly frightened by what he has seen.

In chapter 6, which follows the episode of the boxes, the narrator must
come to terms with another astonishing aspect of the world in which he
finds himself: one of Sergeant Pluck's duties is to steal Michael Gilhaney's
bicycle every Monday, to prevent Gilhaney from becoming a bicycle
himself—a fate to which all cycling inhabitants of the parish are prey.
Pluck explains this situation to the narrator after they have successfully
found the bike where Pluck had hidden it. As all matter is made up of
flying particles known as atoms, it is logical that an exchange of atoms
takes place when, for example, an iron bar is struck with a hammer. Thus
with bicycles and their riders: "[P]eople who spent most of their lives
riding iron bicycles over the rocky roadsteads of the parish get their
personalities mixed up with the personalities of their bicycle . . . [Y]ou
would be surprised at the number of people in these parts who nearly are
half people and half bicycles" (74).

O'Brien makes a great deal of humorous capital out of this notion,
taking it to its furthest conclusion by introducing the idea of sexuality:
"A new lady teacher was here one time with a new bicycle. She was not

very long here till Gilhaney went away into the country on her female bicycle. Can you appreciate the immorality of that?" (77). But the narrator is not amused. Typically, trying to find a touchstone of normality, he tries to avoid confronting the issue: "I would not mind being working this minute on a steamer in the middle of the sea . . . doing the hard manual work. I would like to be far away from here" (74). The reader finds descriptions of the consequences of people-into-bicycles (and bicycles-into-people) funny and diverting, as O'Brien intended he or she should; not so the unfortunate narrator, who learns that riding horses and walking are equally dangerous for the same reason, and says, "My head was packed tight with fears and miscellaneous apprehensions" (78).

Accompanying the policeman to eternity—which is reached by an elevator—compounds the narrator's fears, which are lightened, only to be dashed again before he leaves. He is both tempted and tantalized when MacCruiskeen and Pluck demonstrate a cabinet that will produce unlimited wealth and material. Blocks of gold, as well as a magnifying glass that magnifies to invisibility, are generated and displayed to the incredulous protagonist, who this time becomes calculating instead of terrified: "In the meantime my brain was working coldly and quickly. I ordered a bottle of whiskey, precious stones to the value of £200,000, some bananas, a fountain pen. . . . I remembered other things I had overlooked and ordered underwear, shoes and banknotes, and a box of matches" (118). Cruelly, Pluck provides a bag for removal of the arbitrary selection of goods, and at the narrator's request produces one last item, a weapon "suitable for the pocket which will exterminate any man or any million men who try to take [the narrator's] life" (119). Clearly the narrator has learned little morality in this world, and his punishment is to be given this wealth but to be unable to use it: owing to the physical laws of eternity, nothing can be removed—the elevator that returns them to the outside world will carry only the precise weight it delivered in the first place. The narrator is desolate; he sobs uncontrollably, like a baby; the two policemen (aware of the situation all along) discuss him "in sympathetic undertones as if they were trained doctors in a hospital" (121).

O'Brien's joke rests on an inversion of the familiar expression "You can't take it with you." Far from divesting himself of material things and cultivating a more spiritual frame of mind, the narrator has been in a "heaven" specially designed to punish him for his own greed.

Like MacCruiskeen's boxes, one within another, the narrator moves from "eternity" back to the world of the policemen, and eventually reaches Mathers's house, where he meets the mysterious Policeman Fox—who, frighteningly, has Mathers's face. Fox tells him that the black box he has been searching for contains not cash but "omnium," a priceless substance responsible for the endless display of wealth he witnessed in eternity. In a ghostly state that he himself is unaware of, the narrator returns to the first, "real" world of the novel, in search of Divney and the box.

As O'Brien explained in a letter to William Saroyan, "Although he's [i.e., the narrator] been away for three days, this other fellow is twenty years older and dies of fright when he sees the other lad standing in the door. The two of them walk back along the road again, the first fellow being surprised and frightened just as he was the first time and as if he'd never been through it before. It is made clear that this sort of thing goes on for ever—and there you are."[7] (In the actual published version, the narrator has been dead for 16 years [170].) We are given Divney's speech only as reported by the narrator: "He told me to keep away. He said I was not there. He said I was dead. He said that what he had put under the boards in the big house was not the black box but a mine, a bomb. . . . The house was blown to bits. I was dead" (170).

But the narrator does not know whether or not to believe him, and as he gazes at Divney and his wife, sobbing beside him on the floor, he becomes "uncertain" about them, and instantly appears to forget what he has just been told. He leaves the house, and his mind becomes "completely void": "I did not recall who I was, where I was or what my business was upon earth. I was alone and desolate yet not concerned about myself at all. The eyes in my head were open but they saw nothing because my brain was void" (171). Already our storyteller seems to have lost access to the information he has just been given and is unaware that he has just crossed back from the first to the second world of the text.

Scholarship and Satire

"The main thing to bear in mind is the unimportance of all art. It is very much a minority activity," O'Brien wrote in the *Irish Times* under his Myles na gCopaleen persona. This attitude is one he held throughout his adult life, an attitude curiously combined with the conflicting belief that writing fiction was important. It is true to say that O'Brien reserved his greatest skepticism for the critical industry, particularly that which he saw growing up around Joyce's work; pseudoscholarship and pedantry are pilloried in *The Third Policeman* and *The Hard Life*. In the former work,

O'Brien's narrator describes the profound effect that reading de Selby had on him, so much so that he stole a copy when he left school. Like Prospero, he neglects his affairs and withdraws from the world in the pursuit of study. He produces the definitive "De Selby Index," "wherein the views of all known commentators on every aspect of the savant and his work had been collated. . . . It contained much that was entirely new and proof that many opinions widely held about de Selby and his theories were misconceptions based on misreadings of his work" (12ff.). The book is "so badly needed," in his opinion, that he yields to Divney's temptations and kills Mathers, the second crime he commits in de Selby's name.

De Selby may owe his name to suggestions of the German word *Selbst*, meaning "self." Certainly O'Brien's satire is directed at preoccupation with the self in the sense of idiosyncratic research pursued in a self-regarding manner, with little or no reference to external events or lived experience. Both de Selby and the narrator are guilty of this preoccupation. The narrator recognizes and cites instances where de Selby's theories can only be described as "fantastic" (45) or where his work is so misguided as to be a "regrettable lapse" (19), but he never doubts de Selby's "great mind" (45), even when his own common sense tells him the propositions are ridiculous.

In the narrator, then, we have an example of the worst kind of scholar: obsessively single-minded about the works of a remote and woolly-minded philosopher, and eager to add yet another volume to the existing critical industry surrounding the so-called master. In his reading, the narrator has turned in on himself, taking seriously texts that should have been ridiculed; the result is sterile academic footnoting. So pedantically are the narrator's footnotes presented, however, that *O'Brien's* reader colludes not with narrator but with author, recognizing the "De Selby Index" for what it is—a piece of comic irrelevance. (In certain circles, however, it may generate only uneasy laughter!)

The narrator's preoccupation with scholarship is interesting because, as we have seen, he seems to remember nothing about his former life, not even his own name. Yet he remembers de Selby's, and produces not only chapter and verse but long quotations from de Selby's works. De Selby's theories about the universe, moreover, seem like pale imitations of the apparent logic displayed by the policemen—another paradoxical instance of similarities between the two worlds.

O'Brien's attitude toward modern "academic" criticism is clear in various aspects of his work. It is the basis of his entire mocking stance toward his reader in *At Swim-Two-Birds,* and numerous "Cruiskeen Lawn" columns castigate the inaccuracies of contemporary criticism and its (in his opinion) parasitic nature. The brother in *The Hard Life* (who plundered books in Dublin's National Library more extensively than *At Swim*'s narrator plunders the *Conspectus*) exploits arcane language in the sixpenny leaflets he produces on diverse topics, for example: "It were folly to asseverate that periastral peripatasis on the *aes ductile,* or wire, is destitute of profound peril not only to sundry *membra,* or limbs, but to the back and veriest life itself" (40). *The Third Policeman's* narrator adopts a similar pseudoscholarly style for his academic footnotes, different from his usual narrative voice: "Almost all of the numerous petty litigations in which de Selby was involved afford salutary examples of the humiliations which great minds suffer when forced to have contact with the pedestrian intellects of the unperceiving laity" (128).

Although the footnotes in *The Third Policeman* maintain an ironic relationship with a style of criticism and commentary readers may be familiar with, they do nothing to add an illusion of authenticity to the text—as footnotes in Laclos's *Les Liaisons Dangereuses* are intended to do, for example. In one sense the footnotes in O'Brien's novel function to distract readers' attention from the main business of the narrative, and help to prevent us from recognizing the more fundamental bizarre propositions at work in the book. For example, they occur immediately before the narrator is killed—"My recollections of de Selby were prompted by my visit to the home of old Mr. Mathers" (20)—and throughout the rest of the novel after his death. In one instance de Selby's philosophical theories work by contrast to intensify the concreteness of the reality that is in fact hell. The narrator recalls de Selby's proposition that "a journey is an hallucination"; after a well-documented digression on this topic the narrator returns to his own journey to the police barrack: "I need only say that it was no hallucination. The heat of the sun played incontrovertibly on every inch of me, the hardness of the road was uncompromising" (45). There may even be a reference here to Berkeley's declaration that matter is superfluous and unintelligible and to Dr. Johnson's not unnatural but mistaken belief that he could refute this idea by kicking a stone. De Selby's philosophical questioning of reality is so comic, whimsical, and irrelevant that the fictional world of *The Third Policeman* seems familiar and recognizable by contrast.

The footnotes have one other function within the novel: they unfold a second story, which is connected only tangentially with the murder and subsequent punishment. They do not stand completely alone, but when they are read in conjunction with observations about de Selby in the main text, a second narrative emerges, revealing quarrels, assertions, and counterassertions among de Selby's critics. In this way the novel anticipates Nabokov's *Pale Fire* (1962). A biography of de Selby and the controversy surrounding him is latent in the text, ready to be constructed by the reader.

Before the first chapter begins, historical fact and fiction are placed in a curious relationship to each other by the novel's two epigraphs:

Human existence being an hallucination containing in itself the secondary hallucinations of day and night (the latter an insanitary condition of the atmosphere due to accretions of black air) it ill becomes any man of sense to be concerned at the illusory approach of the supreme hallucination of death.

DE SELBY

Since the affairs of men rest still uncertain,
Let's reason with the worst that can befall.

SHAKESPEARE

Fact and fiction in the persons of Shakespeare and de Selby are equated by the juxtaposition of an actual quotation from a fictional character and an invented one posing as fact. By placing a real and a fictional writer next to each other, O'Brien questions Shakespeare's authenticity as much as he establishes de Selby's. Were it not for the ludicrous phrase in parentheses, the de Selby quotation could plausibly come from any one of a number of mystical-philosophical works. (That "accretions of black air" are responsible for night suggests the once-established belief that night air was dangerous.)

The challenges presented by *The Third Policeman* are very different from those of *At Swim,* and also from those of conventional murder or mystery stories. Here there is no detective figure, and the denouement is not that the murderer is discovered but that he himself is dead. Unreliable narration, realism that is overdetermined, and the use of footnotes all work to distract our attention from this fact. But the work was designed in such a way that it is a palimpsest, revealing in a second reading all that the misguided reader missed the first time. The point of *At Swim* was to engender confusion; *The Third Policeman* encourages it only so that confusion can be conclusively resolved: the reader, eventually, recognizes ways in which the text misled, and is forced to reappraise and to admire O'Brien's virtuosity. In *At Swim-Two-Birds* O'Brien was content to have the private satisfaction of feeling sure that his novel would elude (and delude) most readers, with its promise of systems that in fact remains unfulfilled. From this point in his writing career onward, O'Brien becomes less innovative and more straightforward in his writing.

Chapter Four
An Béal Bocht
(The Poor Mouth)

It is difficult for someone like me to be so presumptuous as to discuss two major works of Irish literature written in Irish, when I can read them only in translation. Even authors' names and the titles of books prove to be a problem. The fact that O'Brien held the English translation of *An tOileánach (The Islandman)* in contempt and was dead before his own *An Béal Bocht* was translated by Patrick Power intensifies the problems. For the purposes of this chapter I refer to Tomás Ó Criomhthain by the Anglicized vesion of his name, Ó Crohan, and to his book as *The Islandman. An Béal Bocht* is, in English, *The Poor Mouth,* an expression that refers to "making a pretence of being poor or in bad circumstances in order to gain advantage for oneself from creditors or prospective creditors."[1] The book was published in 1941 under the pseudonym "Myles na gCopaleen," but I shall continue to refer to "O'Brien" throughout.

The Poor Mouth[2] is a fictional autobiographical account of a life of rural poverty. It is a comic novel in its own right, but many of its effects are intensified if one is aware of the background of rural autobiography on which it at least partly depends.

In his "Cruiskeen Lawn" column O'Brien wrote that Ó Crohan's *The Islandman* was "the superbest of all books I have ever read. It's sheer greatness is a lesson for all." He continues, "The book was published about 1930 and disturbed myself so much that I put it away, a thing not to be seen or thought about and certainly not to be discussed with strangers. But its impact was explosive. In one week I wrote a parody of it called *An Béal Bocht.*"[3] It is important to recognize that the comedy in *The Poor Mouth* is not directed at Ó Crohan's work, which O'Brien clearly regards with a feeling not far short of reverence.

"*An tOileánach* is literature," O'Brien wrote. "There is no book (of ours or of any other tribe) in English comparable to it. And it is not the 'speech of the people' or the 'nice idioms' that confer the nobility of literature on it. The genuine authoritative human stuff is there, it is artistic, it moves the reader to tears or laughter as the author chooses."[4] Our ideas of parody have to be adjusted, for it was clearly not O'Brien's intention to denigrate *The Islandman*. He was so deeply affected— "disturbed"—by the book that his comedy is more likely to have been a cathartic exercise for his own feelings: if its effect was so powerful that it was "not to be seen or thought about" and certainly not to be discussed with strangers, then the creative energy it inspired had to be directed toward other ends. O'Brien calls *The Poor Mouth* a "prolonged sneer" and adds, "My prayer is that all who read it afresh will be stimulated into stumbling upon the majestic book on which it is based."

The preface to the *The Poor Mouth*—written by O'Brien—claims that his part in the account was purely editorial: "This document is exactly as I received it from the author's hand except that much of the original matter had to be omitted due to pressure of space and to the fact that improper subjects were included in it." The "author," Bonaparte O'Coonassa, we are told, "is still alive today safe in jail and free from the miseries of life"; the implication is that life in prison is comfortable compared with life in Corkadoragha—where the rain pours down incessantly and where there is little to distinguish the lives of human beings from those of the pigs, both species sharing not only an unrelieved diet of potatoes but living quarters as well.

The device of the editor preparing authentic papers that have come into his or her possession is part of a time-honored literary tradition. Defoe's *Robinson Crusoe, Journal of the Plague Year,* and *Moll Flanders* are supposedly "firsthand" accounts, and Laclos claims only to have edited the letters that form *Les Liaisons Dangereuses*. But the fiction of authenticity that is conferred in such cases is, in *The Poor Mouth,* evoked merely for the pleasure of sending it up.

Ó Crohan's was a real autobiographical account of his life in the isolated Blasket Islands off the west coast of Ireland. He was born in 1856, the youngest of five children in a family whose living was made, as was that of the rest of the small island community, from farming and fishing. Maire Cruise O'Brien says that life on the Great Blasket "in the last half of the last century was a survival probably unique in Europe; it was the survival of a living community only barely touched by the industrial revolution."[6]

Until he was 18, Ó Crohan attended school intermittently, whenever a teacher was sent over from the mainland. But young women teachers tended to leave to marry; men did not stay long either; and so school was infrequent, sometimes punctuated by gaps of a couple of years. Teaching was in English, and Ó Crohan was unable to read or write Irish, his own language, until his interest in learning these skills was generated in late middle age. Ó Crohan had no literary aspirations but was prompted to record his life by the interest of visitors to the area, such as Brian O'Kelly (who edited *The Islandman*), Carl Marstrander ("The Norseman"), and Robin Flower, (who translated *The Islandman* into English). It is this Gaelic League kind of interest in Irish language and culture—an interest that could be seen as patronizing—which O'Brien consistently parodied in his "Cruiskeen Lawn" column. Enthusiasm has a habit of turning into fanaticism, and the lives of the people of the rural community were often romanticized and idealized by these urban dwellers.

O'Brien was particularly scathing about Flower's translation of Ó Crohan's work, not because the use of English is poor but at least partly because, as Cyril O Ceiran says, "Anybody reading the book might well be lured into accepting that Tomás Ó Criomhthain was an English-speaker, was in fact an inhabitant of an island off the west coast of England."

O'Brien translated several passages from *The Islandman* in "Cruiskeen Lawn," and a comparison of these with Flower's translation says a great deal about O'Brien's desire to represent the rhythms and complexities of Irish language. The differences between the first passage quoted below, by Flower, and the second, by O'Brien, shows the latter's concerns and the way in which he laughed at them:

It was holiday time with us for a while after that, and it was a fine calm year. The big boats were bringing home quantities of fish. The three of them were full to the brim every day. As my father and Pats had two men's share, we always had a fine show of fish in the little house.

That was the first time, I think that I ceased to be a spoilt darling, for my sides were sore that day from carrying fish home in a bag on my back. Each man of the crew had a thousand fish, so that made two thousand for us. My father said that I carried more than a thousand home.[8]

We had easy times then for a while, and the year that was in it, she was a fine quiet one. A lot of fish were being brought in in the big boats. The three boats were full to the tops, a day. Owing to the force of two men—my father and Patrick—being at us, there was a fine sight of it in the cabin. That was the first day of mine, I think, completely separated from being a mollycoddle, because a hard straining was taken out of my sides pulling the fish to the house with me in a bag beyant on my back. A thousand fish had each single man on that particular

day. That left two thousand to us. My father said that I had brought a thousand
and more of them home.[9]

O'Brien's translation cannot be taken entirely at face value. It is as likely
that he was parodying Flower's English as much as he was offering an
alternative. English words are being used, but certainly not in grammati-
cal order or with any real clarity. The passage as rendered by O'Brien
illustrates the difficulties of translation and certainly reminds us that we
are not reading about a remote corner of England. Flower's English is
undoubtedly less of a strain to assimilate. *The Islandman* is a long book,
and it must be said that Ó Crohan's work reached a wider audience by
virtue of Flower's translation.

For O'Brien, *The Islandman* is "the symbol of a Gaelic order gone
under for good."[10] In *The Poor Mouth* his laughter and scorn are poured on
the enthusiasts who want to revive the culture and language but have no
real understanding of or feeling for them. His satire gains from the way it
is presented: through the eyes of the naive narrator, an inhabitant of
Corkadoragha. Because of its remoteness and therefore its inbuilt
resistance to change, Corkadoragha has become an object of interest for
the Gaelic League: "Oftentimes now there were gentlemen to be seen
about the roads, some young and others aged, addressing the poor Gaels
in awkward unintelligible Gaelic and delaying them on their way to the
field. . . . That is how the group, called the Gaeligores nowadays, came
to Corkadoragha for the first time. They rambled about the countryside
with little black notebooks for a long time before the people noticed that
they were not *peelers* [police officers] but gentle-folk endeavouring to learn
the Gaelic of our ancestors and ancients." (48–49).

O'Brien's satire is nearly always on a grand scale, making its point by
gross exaggeration. But there are still some points made with more
subtlety for readers to work out for themselves. More visitors flock to
Corkadoragha each year, until "the advent of spring was no longer judged
by the flight of the first swallow but by the first Gaeligore seen on the
roads" (49). It is understatement here that emphasizes the fact that the
eager visitors are not so eager that they would brave winter weather in
order to discover and celebrate their heritage.

When the interest begins to fall off, the narrator's grandfather, "the
Old-Grey-Fellow," organizes a *feis,* or festival. His aims are purely
financial, for the visitors inevitably spent money in Corkadoragha when
they were there, and as their interest wanes, so does the small extra cash
flow. Crowds, carefully attired for the occasion, flock in from Galway and

Dublin for the *feis*. Strange sights greet the locals. There is, for example, "a fellow without any breeches on him but wearing a lady's underskirt instead. It was stated that such as he wore Gaelic costume and, if this was correct, what a peculiar change came in your appearance as a result of a few Gaelic words in your head!" Traditional costume, of course, is unknown to the local inhabitants: "There were men present wearing a simple unornamented dress—these, I thought, had little Gaelic; others had such nobility, style and elegance in their feminine attire that it was evident that their Gaelic was fluent" (51). The narrator, underlining his own inevitable and innate affinities with the community he lives in, fails completely and comically to recognize the ignorant enthusiasm of the visitors: "I felt quite ashamed that there was not even one true Gael among us in Corkadoragha." The ironies are all O'Brien's, not the narrator's.

The Gaelic enthusiasts make the naive narrator even more aware of Corkadoragha's inadequacies by taking names from the natural environment in imitation of the heroes of myth and legend. They assume titles like "The Bold Horse," "The Branchy Tree," and "The West Wind." O'Brien includes in his long list such ludicrous names as "Popeye the Sailor" and "The Dative Case" to emphasize the affectation; he merely feels that the inhabitants' given and surnames are yet another indication that they have lost their true Gaelicism.

There is a real split between (a) those whose lives have suddenly become the object of interest and research and (b) the completely unromantic hardship of that way of life. The president of the *feis* makes a long speech in which virtually every third word is *Gaelic*—"We are all Gaelic Gaels of Gaelic lineage" (54)—and during which "many of the native Gaels were becoming feeble from standing because their legs were debilitated from lack of nourishment" (55). Nothing could bring out the discrepancy between romantic idealization and actual fact as clearly as this scene.

The visitors, so anxious to address the "poor Gaels in awkward and unintelligible Gaelic" delay them "on their way to the fields" (48). This action is one that Ó Crohan mentions in passing in *The Islandman,* and there is something faintly comic in the idea of his working hard to keep body and soul together during the day and turning his mind to questions put by the likes of Marstrander during the evening: "It was after the day's work was done that I used to go to him, for the nights were long at that time of the year. We were fishing and I had a boat with another man and that wouldn't permit me to spend any time in his company that would

interfere with the fishing." Yet, Marstrander was pushed too, and asked
Ó Crohan for more time. "How could I give the gentleman a refusal?"
writes Ó Crohan. "I told him I'd do my best for him. So we went at it
together, and, whenever I came in for my dinner, I would go to him, and
that wouldn't set me back in my fishing for long." [11] While he had his
health and strength, Ó Crohan had no choice but to put physical work
first; recalling and recording life and work always had to be subordinate.
Such honest unpretentiousness makes *The Islandman* the remarkable
document it is.

Peter O'Leary's *My Story* is another autobiographical work O'Brien
had in mind when he wrote *The Poor Mouth*. O'Leary differed from Ó
Crohan in that he, like O'Brien, was brought up to be bilingual: "I had
both English and Gaelic from the cradle."[12] Not only that, but his
mother taught him French from an early age, and training for the
priesthood later in life, he learned Latin and Greek. *My Story* was written
when Father O'Leary was in his seventies; it was published in 1915 and
was the inspiration behind many such autobiographical accounts.
O'Brien refers to the book in *The Poor Mouth* when the Old-Grey-Fellow
asks a Gaeligore why Corkadoragha's Gaelic has declined: "I don't think
that Father Peter has the word *decline* in any of his works," the Gaeligore
courteously replies (49).

In the last chapter of *The Islandman* Ó Crohan sets down his reasons for
writing his book: "I have written minutely of much that we did, for it
was my wish that somewhere there should be a memorial of it all, and I
have done my best to set down the character of the people about me so
that some record of us might live after us, for the like of us will never be
seen again."[13] This is O'Brien's starting point: "I am noting down the
matters which are in this document because the next life is approaching
me swiftly . . . and also because our likes will never be there again. It is
right and fitting that some testimony of the diversions and adventures of
our lives should be provided for those who succeed us because our types
will never be there again" (11). Ó Crohan's phrase "the like of us will
never be seen again," which he uses only once, is repeated unmercifully
throughout *The Poor Mouth*. Not amusing in itself, it accrues comic
overtones by repetition, the elegiac qualities made redundant by the
reader's sense that it is really just as well!

Like the first-person narrator of *The Third Policeman*, Bonaparte had, by
his own account, a bizarre childhood. But this fact is easier to understand
in the context of *The Poor Mouth*, because apparently surreal qualities can
be clarified by reference to *The Islandman*. Thus, when Bonaparte tells of

his birth, he says, "My father never expected me because he was a quiet fellow and did not understand very accurately the ways of life. . . . The people said that my mother was not expecting me either and it is a fact that the whisper went around that I was not born of my mother at all but of another woman" (13). He cannot resist adding that this idea is in fact neighbors' gossip that can no longer be checked, as they are all dead "and their likes will not be there again." His humor in the passage is characteristic. He has taken a remark of Ó Crohan's—"nobody expected me at all when I came their way"[14]—and elaborated it to its absurd "logical" conclusion. Ó Crohan's birth was "unexpected" because he was much the youngest of six children, after a gap of seven or eight years. But there is also a satiric glance here at prudery in certain areas of modern Irish literature—modesty and reticence that were certainly not endemic to earlier Irish writing or folklore. In a letter written on 16 April 1941 O'Brien says that in his revision of *The Poor Mouth* he has "cut out completely all reference to 'sexual matter' and made every other change necessary to render the text completely aseptic and harmless. . . . I am satisfied that the thing is now safe from puritanical objection."

The description of Bonaparte's mother owes a great deal to Ó Crohan's description of his parents: "My father was a middle-sized man, stout and strong. My mother was a flourishing woman, tall as a peeler, strong, vigorous and lively, with bright shining hair. [15] This portrayal is given a comic aspect in *The Poor Mouth* when Bonaparte tells us that though he was "very young at the time he was born," after six months, wisdom began to come, and from his cradle he observed that his mother was "a decent, hefty, big-boned woman, a silent, cross, big-breasted woman" (14). The vocabulary and the narrative stance comically debunk Joyce's imitation of a child's register of vocabulary at the beginning of *A Portrait of the Artist as a Young Man.*

Ó Crohan describes his life as one of hard work and industry; Bonaparte, like all O'Brien's protagonists, is idle. O'Brien's parodic effects are gained sometimes by wild exaggeration, sometimes by contradiction.

One of the most moving things about Ó Crohan's autobiography is the evident emotional restraint in discussing his private life—his marriage, the births and deaths of his children, and the death of his wife. We take it as read that the understatement, the fact that he does not dwell on his feelings, is no indication that these are lacking (by contrast, Defoe's Robinson Crusoe marries, has children, and disposes of them all in one paragraph, without mentioning their names, right at the end of the novel). Chapters of Ó Crohan's book are devoted to descriptions of fishing expeditions or days spent in the fields; a great deal of worry is expended over a dog lost down a rabbit hole. But we never learn his wife's name, or the names of most of his children: "Ten children were born to us, but they had no good fortune, God help us. The very first of them that we christened was only seven or eight years old when he fell over the cliff and was killed. From that time on they went as quickly as they came. Two died of measles, and every epidemic that came carried off one or the other of them."[16] "All these things," Ó Crohan says, "were a sore trouble to the poor mother, and she, too, was taken from me." His own feelings we must take for granted: "May God's blessing be with them—those of them that are in the grave—and with the poor woman whose heart broke for them."[17] Much later he tells us that he was "completely upset and muddled" after his wife's death, and refers to the "low spirits" he was unable to overcome.[18] These are the only references, but we do not infer that because they are apparently marginalized, his emotional distress was concomitant. Rather, they assume the status and dignity of private grief not to be exhibited for public examination.

O'Brien's treatment of Bonaparte's marriage and fatherhood is undoubtedly marginalized for very different reasons: to show the emotional limitation of the character—naive and stupid, as condescending literary representations of Irish peasants tend to be. Marriage and the birth and death of child and wife are recounted and dismissed in one chapter; for different reasons they take up about the same space as Ó Crohan devotes to his family life. Mabel, Bonaparte's wife, wants to return to her father's house after her wedding, and so Bonaparte's mother sits on her to prevent her escape, and endeavors "to make her see reason . . . informing her that it is compulsory to submit to Gaelic fate" (84).

Returning from Galway one night, about a year later, Bonaparte notices that there is a new piglet in the house; on closer examination it turns out to be a baby boy. He is christened Leonard, but "Alas! happiness is not lasting and neither is joy for any Gaelic pauper because he does not escape for long the scourging of fate" (86). When he is a year and a day old, the child's face suddenly turns gray and he starts coughing. Bonaparte runs to fetch his wife, only to find her "cold in death . . . her mouth wide open while the pigs snorted round her." Leonard is lifeless too by the time Bonaparte gets back to him. "Here then, reader," he comments, "is some evidence for you of the life of the Gaelic paupers in Corkadoragha and an account of the fate that awaits them from their first day" (87). He concludes the chapter with a platitude: "After great merriment comes sorrow and good weather never remains for ever." It is comically inappropriate not least because there was never any indication of "merriment"—other than the delight O'Brien takes in telling his tale of poverty and deprivation.

Courtship is carried out according to the way it has been conducted in the stories of Séamus Ó Grianna. The inhabitants of Corkadoragha are now bound by *literary* traditions; thus when Bonaparte goes to claim Mabel's hand and is eager to "settle the deal and get our evening spuds," his grandfather rebukes him: "I'm afraid that you don't understand the world. 'Tis said in the good books that describe the affairs of Gaelic paupers that it's in the middle of the night that two men come visiting if they have a five-noggin bottle and are looking for a woman. Therefore we must sit here until the middle of the night comes" (81). Bonaparte objects that they will be soaked to the skin, but the Old Fellow tells him, "There's no use for us trying to escape from fate."

The episode in which Bonaparte goes to school and in which he, like all his fellow pupils, is told that his name is "Jams O Donnell" is an exaggeration of Séamus Ó Grianna's "Caisleáin Óir," in which the young boy fails to recognize the Anglicized version of his Irish name on his first day at school but has it imposed upon him anyway. O'Brien's range of reference is wide; one reviewer of *The Poor Mouth* wrote, "There is hardly a book written in our language in the last twenty years, or before, that he does not assail. He calls them 'good books.'"[19]

In *The Poor Mouth* O'Brien sends up received ideas of the Irish peasant as unfeeling, uneducated, and stupid. Ó Crohan describes the conditions in which he was brought up, sharing the cottage with hens and sheep that were brought in at night. Not to be outdone, O'Brien introduces pigs into Bonaparte's hovel, with graphic descriptions of the smell they generate—to the extent that Bonaparte, his mother, and his grandfather are obliged to sleep outdoors until the death of one exceptionally large pig, which also happens to suffer from an illness. When a visiting school inspector suggests that living in such close quarters with the animals is "shameful, improper and a very bad thing" (20) and that it might be a good idea to build a hut at the side of the house to extend the accommodations, the family seizes on the idea with a will. Within a week, with the (traditional!) help of neighbors, the hut is completed: "But alas! things are not what they seem to be! When I, my grandmother and two of my brothers had spent two nights in the hut, we were so cold and drenched wet that it is a wonder we did not die straight away and we couldn't get any relief until we went back to the house and were comfortable again among the cattle" (20). They fail to grasp the point entirely. O'Brien's satire is directed not at peasants but at unflattering literary representations of them.

The Poor Mouth is a comic novel in much the same sense as The Third Policeman is. The miseries of life are as unrelenting as the rain that teems down; there is no escape from unalleviated malign fate. As the unnamed narrator of The Third Policeman is doomed to repeat his nightmare, so Bonaparte is destined to continue his limited existence with no possibility of change. That man is a victim, at the mercy of the unkind elements, is made abundantly clear throughout, as, for example, when Bonaparte describes one particular night as "the most nocturnal night I ever knew because of the quantity of rain and the blackness of the black-darkness"; the comic tautology has a sinister quality too. Bonaparte treks across the countryside, "the venomous wind tearing [him] and the squalls of rain belting the crown of [his] head abominably" (116). Brendan Kelly sums up the tragic dimension: "Throughout the book, the elements blast down on the heads of everybody, man and beast alike. What strikes the reader is the *relentless* nature of this oppression, the fierce tireless energy of its tyranny. Myles na gCopaleen [O'Brien] sees man as a sort of target for the fury of nature. . . . I can't help feeling that this black vision sometimes transcends the satirical purpose it so brilliantly serves, and achieves at certain moments a real tragic intensity."[20] There is no escape from this fate of battling with the elements, no scope for individuals to overcome circumstances.

The similarities with The Third Policeman are more specifically apparent at the end of The Poor Mouth, when Bonaparte tries unsuccessfully to rise above his Gaelic misery—not by murdering, as the Third Policeman's narrator does, but by committing robbery of a kind. The result is similar. The Old Fellow tells Bonaparte that, strange as it may seem, the present unremitting rain was even worse when his grandfather was young: "Whoever couldn't swim well, went off to heaven" (101). The weather was so "sky-crucifying" that at one time everyone in the countryside was drowned, except for Maeldoon O'Poenassa, who escaped by boat from Corkadoragha and, rather like Noah in the ark, came to rest on the top of a mountain, since known as "Hunger-stack." There he remained, the way down being too steep when the waters receded.

Bonaparte resolves that he will reach the top of the mountain in order to retrieve the plundered fortune that O'Poenassa reputedly took with him: "I was of the opinion that one might be better off seeking death searching for the good life on Hunger-stack than suffering hard times for ever in Corkadoragha. It were better for a man to die on the mountain from celestial water than to live at home famished in the centre of the plain" (103).

The miseries of his journey are unrelieved, rain "bursting out of the sky in such profusion that it terrified me and injured the crown of my head" (104). Floodwaters bear down on him too, bringing with them "trees, large stones and small farms of land" (105). Eventually he reaches the summit and is horrified by the sight of O'Poenassa, who appears to be dead—as indeed he should be, given the natural order of things and the fact that he was stranded there at least four generations earlier. Bonaparte retains his sanity by focusing on the matter at hand: gathering together the gold and precious stones that lay scattered around.

The situation recalls that of the narrator in *The Third Policeman*, searching for Mathers's black box and suddenly becoming aware that Mathers is not only present but observing him. In much the same way, Bonaparte, realizing that the fire that burns in the cave must be tended by someone, is overcome by fear and tries to find out whether O'Poenassa is alive. He throws a stone, which strikes the withered old man with no visible effect, and remarks to himself, half-aloud, "He has nothing to say." This statement is contradicted when the "corpse" replies, "And what narrative would give you pleasure?" (109), striking terror into Bonaparte's heart.

Bonaparte does not stay for an extended colloquy, such as that Mathers has with the narrator in *The Third Policeman*. But in much the same way, O'Poenassa speaks in his own register, which has no reference to Bonaparte's. No real dialogue or communication would be possible between them. Here Power's footnote to his translation indicates that O'Brien employed a form of Gaelic used during A.D. 1000–1250 for O'Poenassa's speech.

Bonaparte escapes, and duly returns to Corkadoragha, burying his gold and living for a year with his secret; there is nothing he wants to buy with it: "It was a hard, impossible task. I thought first of buying foodstuffs but since I had tasted nothing except for fish and potatoes, it was unlikely that the variety of foods consumed by the gentle-folk of Dublin would agree with me even if I had the opportunity of buying them or even knew their names!" (112). No clothing would stand up to the rigors of the climate without rotting, and Bonaparte finds himself in the position of being "sunk in poverty, half-dead from hunger and hardship," yet failing to think of "any pleasant useful object" that he needs. Eventually he decides

to buy a pair of boots, which purchase requires a westward journey to find
a town with a suitable shop. When he has acquired them, he is unable to
wear them, for boots have not been seen in Corkadoragha since the *feis*
and would attract attention, ridicule, and mockery. He buries them, as he
did the gold, and on the one occasion when he does put them on, secretly
and at dead of night, he feels a certain satisfaction. But that sense of
gratification is slender, for it is only "foot-squeezing, tormenting and
foot-hurt I received from them" (116).

An English-speaking policeman arrives in Corkadoragha, investigating
a murder that took place in Galway. The Old Fellow translates the
officer's stream of English for Bonaparte's benefit: "He's saying . . . that
some scoundrel murdered a gentleman in Galway lately and that he stole a
lot of gold pieces from him. He says that you were buying things with
gold a while ago and he says that you're to lay out all you have in your
pocket on the table" (119). The 19 pieces of gold in Bonaparte's pocket
convict him circumstantially of a murder he did not commit; the
impossibilities of communication are multiplied, for Bonaparte under-
stands nothing of his interrogation or trial. It is only while he is at a
railway station, about to be conveyed to jail, that he sees another pauper of
similar appearance to his own, a person who explains to him what his fate
is to be: 29 years' imprisonment. Bonaparte faints, and only the application of a bucket of water—doubtless reminding him of the reality of
existence in Corkadoragha!—brings him around. It is then that he sees an
old man, "bent and broken and as thin as a stem of grass" (123).
Bonaparte asks, "Phwat is yer nam?" and is told, "Jams O'Donnell":
"Wonder and joy swept over me," Bonaparte says, "as flashes of lightning
out of the celestial sky. I lost my voice and I nearly lost my senses again.
My father! my own father!! my own little father!!! my kinsman, my
progenitor, my friend!!!! We devoured one another with our eyes eagerly
and I offered him my hand" (124).

His father—if indeed it is his father—has just served 29 years in the
same prison Bonaparte is destined for. Thus O'Brien achieves a circularity
similar to that of *The Third Policeman,* in this case with the next
generation doomed to repeat the miseries of the preceding one. Conversation is impossible; the two men exchange only "eerie staring" and a
minimum of words. "Yes! that was the first time that I laid eyes on my
father and that he laid eyes on me; one wee moment at the station and
then—separation for ever. Certainly I suffered Gaelic hardship throughout my life—distress, need, ill-treatment, adversity, calamity, foul play,

misery, famine and ill-luck. I do not think my like will be there again!"
(125).

Although *The Poor Mouth* owes a good part of its existence to
contemporary interest in Gaelic autobiography, O'Brien has achieved
much more than a straightforward parody or satire of such works. In the
bleakness of the hard life that he so comically recounts are the seeds of
his own black humor that inform both *The Third Policeman* and *At
Swim-Two-Birds*. The difficulty, if not total impossibility, of communication, together with the essential isolation of the individual, is particularly
appropriate in the context of a native language that is understood only by
a very small percentage of the population. O'Brien himself summed up
his attitude to the Gaelic fanatics when he wrote to Sean O'Casey:

I am much obliged for your recent letter regarding the "Béal Bocht." . . . It is by
no means all you say but it is an honest attempt to get under the skin of a certain
type of "Gael," which I find the most nauseating phenomenon in Europe. I
mean the baby-brained dawnburst brigade who are ignorant of everything,
including the Irish language itself. I'm sure they were plentiful enough in your
own day. I cannot see any real prospect of reviving Irish at the present rate of
going and way of working. I agree absolutely with you when you say it is
essential, particularly for any sort of a literary worker. It supplies that unknown
quantity in us that enables us to transform the English language and this seems
to hold off people who know little or no Irish, like Joyce. It seems to be an inbred
thing.[21]

Irish may be useful for the artist, who needs a specific awareness of the
ways in which language works; however, as a medium of common speech
to be imposed on a people who have already largely lost it, Irish is
redundant.

Chapter Five
The Hard Life

O'Brien started writing *The Hard Life* in 1960.[1] It is subtitled "An Exegesis of Squalor," and he dedicated it to Graham Greene, who more than 20 years earlier had recommended that Longman publish *At Swim-Two-Birds*. Instead of inserting the usual disclaimer found at the start of a novel, O'Brien makes an outrageous claim at the beginning of this work: "All the persons in this book are real and none is fictitious even in part." Thus both the fiction and the comedy begin before the first chapter. Incongruity always delighted O'Brien, and he wrote to congratulate the publisher on its production of the book: "It is precisely right that elegance should attach to a volume which contains a treatise on piss and vomit."[2]

Like *At Swim-Two-Birds* and *The Third Policeman*, *The Hard Life* is a first-person narration; this time, however, the narrator does—eventually —tell us his name. In the second chapter the two boys, brothers, are introduced to their uncle as Manus and Finbarr, "fine Irish names" (16), but it is not until the third chapter that we learn Manus is the older brother, Finbarr the narrator. Given names are used very little, the narrator referring to his brother more often than not as "the brother." Finbarr is scarcely more personable than the protagonists of the earlier books; as O'Brien said, "The 'I,' narrator or interlocutor, is himself a complete ass."[3] He is also less interesting than his predecessors, being neither a writer nor dead.

The opening of *The Hard Life* has much in common with the opening of *The Third Policeman*. Finbarr looks back on his childhood with similar lack of emotion: "It is not that I half knew my mother. I knew half of her: the lower half—her lap, legs, feet, her hands and wrists as she bent forward. At the time, of course, I was very young. Then one day she did not seem to be there any more. So far as I knew she had gone away without a word, no goodbye or goodnight. A while afterwards I asked my brother, five years my senior, where the mammy was" (11). The mother is acutely observed from the child's very limited perspective. He has been given no information about her death, and though he is, of course, older and wiser when he tells this story, the naive narrative stance is maintained throughout the childhood section. His brother tells him that she has "gone to a better land":

—Will she be back?
—I don't think so.
—Mean to say we'll never see her again?
—I don't think we will. She is staying with the old man.

Manus's reference to "the old man" typifies his skepticism—developed throughout the novel—about religion, but Finbarr's response to the news is more interesting. Retrospectively at least, Finbarr expresses no feeling at all, not even exhibiting a sense of selfish loss: "At the time I found all this very vague and unsatisfying." We come to expect lack of emotion in O'Brien's fiction, however, and would be surprised to find emotion. O'Brien's dark comic view of the world has something in common with Beckett's: on the whole, characters inhabit an absurd universe in which things happen to them, rather than their showing any control over their destinies.

That there is no father to speak of emphasizes a curious lack of family in any of O'Brien's novels: *At Swim's* protagonist lives with an uncle, *The Third Policeman's* narrator's parents are equally absent, and Finbarr and Manus are brought up by an uncle. Although lack of family life in O'Brien's fiction could perhaps be seen as a contributory factor in the characters' alienation, it is more likely that O'Brien is alluding to the fact that heroes of novels rarely have parents—Heathcliff in *Wuthering Heights,* for example, or Pip in *Great Expectations.* Heroes are usually brought up by unsympathetic relatives, and their real backgrounds are shrouded, as Heathcliff's are, in mystery. It is this romantic notion which O'Brien parodies—his protagonists have all the right criteria for becoming remarkable men, but they all fail.

Finbarr's father is represented only by a photograph: "a stern upright figure wearing great moustaches and attired in a uniform with a large peaked cap. I could never make out what the uniform stood for. He might have been a field-marshal or an admiral, or just an orderly officer in the fire brigade; indeed, he might have been a postman" (11). This description is amusing, but it also compounds the effect of uncertain family background: Finbarr gives us biographical information, but quite deliberately from a limited, childhood perspective, even though the account is a retrospective one. We are still unaware, then, at this stage, whether the "hard life" of the title refers to poverty, or misfortune, or indeed whether it is satiric in tone.

"Everything was done with deliberation," O'Brien wrote to his agent, [4] "the characters illuminating themselves and each other by their outlandish behaviour and preposterous conversations." This applies mainly to Mr. Collopy's and Father Fahrt's conversations, but Manus's recollections of his mother, centering on the superiority of her cooking to Annie's (the girl who comes in to look after the two boys), are an example. Manus's deprivation is expressed not in terms of lost love or affection but in the substitution of Annie's greasy meatballs for wholesome food.

In 1890, when Finbarr is about five years old, the two boys are removed from Annie's sole care and taken to Washington Place, near the canal in Dublin. They are to be brought up by Mr. Collopy, their mother's half-brother. Annie is his daughter by his first marriage, though by the time the boys move in, he is married to Mrs. Crotty. The couple always address each other by their formal titles: "An ill-disposed person might suspect that they were not married at all and that Mrs. Crotty was a kept woman or resident prostitute. But that is quite unthinkable, if only because of Mr. Collopy's close interest in the Church in matters of doctrine and dogma, and also his friendship with the German priest from Leeson Street, Father Kurt Fahrt, S.J., who was a frequent caller" (18). The aspersions cast on Mr. Collopy and Mrs. Crotty's married state are typical of the sense of sordidness that underlies the novel. The foster parents are of an unprepossessing appearance, and in the fourth chapter Mrs. Crotty takes to her bed because of ill health. We are never told precisely what is wrong with her, but she dies and in some way her sickness is bound up with Mr. Collopy's mission in life. This mission is never clearly stated, voluble though Collopy is on the subject, but eventually the reader realizes that it has to do with providing public lavatories for women in Dublin. The subject is hardly hilarious, and it must be said that O'Brien's sense of humor failed him somewhat in this instance. What comedy there is can only be found in the passionate intensity with which Mr. Collopy pursues his course, coupled with his prudishness in never openly mentioning it. "Do you not think that women have enough suffering, as you call it, bringing babies into the world?" he asks Father Fahrt. "And why do they do that? Is it because they're mad to sanctify themselves? Well faith no! It's because the husband is one great torch ablaze with the fires of lust!" (30).

Father Fahrt insists that sexual intercourse and thus procreation are the right of the married man and his duty for the greater glory of God: they are not only right but natural. Mr. Collopy seizes on this point: "Then tell me this. Is the other business natural?" "Other business" is, of course, a euphemism for the evacuation of bodily waste products—a polite way of putting it that undoubtedly would have helped Mr. Collopy out, had he thought of it! "Certainly," the priest replies. "Our bodies are sacred temples. It is a function." States Mr. Collopy: "Very well. What name have you for the dirty ignoramuses who more or less ban that function? . . . Right well you know I have the trotters wore off me going up the stairs of that filthy Corporation begging them, telling them, ordering them to do something" (30).

Mr. Collopy claims that the Lord Mayor and "the other gougers in the City Hall" are "*killing* unfortunate women" (32) by failing to provide lavatories. He attributes Mrs. Crotty's death at least partly to the same cause: "I will not say . . . that what-you-know was the sole reason for the woman's demise. Not the *sole* reason, mind you. But Christ it had plenty to do with it" (50). And again: "Only the Almighty knows how many unfortunate women would be brought to an early grave. . . . [T]he worry and trouble of it might even bring myself there" (51).

O'Brien might appear to be showing an unusual sympathy with women's welfare, but the text does not stand up to any form of feminist examination. Sympathy with women in this instance in fact serves the opposite function, because Mr. Collopy's obsession makes him ridiculous. Women are as absent in *The Hard Life* as they are in all of O'Brien's fiction. Mrs. Crotty is hardly a presence in the novel, because her illness confines her to her bedroom. When she is seen, her appearance is unsettling: "She had taken to the bed two months before and insisted that the door between her bedroom and the kitchen should be always left slightly ajar so that her cries, often faint, could be heard either by Mr. Collopy or Annie. Neither myself nor the brother ever entered the room but all the same I had accidentally seen her on several occasions . . . clutching the bannister with one frail hand, her robe or nightdress of fantastic shape and colour and a frightening pallor on her spent face" (24). Mrs. Crotty is certainly a product of the "hard life." With the exception of the boys, none of the characters are fit and healthy; even Father Fahrt suffers from psoriasis, a skin ailment that causes itching and, inevitably, scratching. Mr. Collopy himself takes ill and dies before the end of the book.

Against this background of illness and obsession, the two boys are educated and grow up. Finbarr is 16 by the end of the book. The boys are sent to different schools, Manus to the Christian Brothers on Westland Row, Finbarr to Synge Street. O'Brien, as usual, is satiric at the expense of formal education. On Finbarr's first morning, Brother Gaskett says he

will teach him everything from "the three Rs to Euclid and Aristopha-
nes." But although Finbarr's evenings are spent toiling over endless
homework, the only thing he actually tells us he learns about is "the
leather," "a strap of the kind used on bags. It is a number of such straps
sewn together to form a thing of great thickness that is nearly as rigid as a
club but just sufficiently flexible to prevent the breaking of the bones of
the hand. Blows of it . . . to the top of the thumb or wrist, conferred
immediate paralysis followed by agony as the blood tried to get back to
the afflicted part" (22). Apart from the immense amount of homework
the boys are given, and the fact that a system of "cogging," or copying,
each other's work exists, this is all we learn of Manus and Finbarr's
education. "The brother" is clearly intelligent and lives by his wits,
reserving only scorn for the education he has received.

One day, coming home from school, Finbarr is terrified at the sight of
his brother, apparently walking on air, head and shoulders above a tallish
tree in the front garden: "Thoroughly scared, I thought of Another who
had walked on water" (23). The explanation is not quite so outrageous,
however—Manus, now aged 16, has taught himself high-wire walking.
Acquiring a sense of balance, he tells Finbarr, is mere child's play; the
only difficulty to be overcome is "what they call psychological. It's a new
word but I know what it means" (25). Given that the year is only 1906, it
is clear that Manus has done some research on his own account; but his
endeavor is always directed toward self-interest and money-making.
Under the pseudonym of Professor Latimer Dodds—"a retired trapeze
and high wire artist"—he sells a course of postal tuition in that art at
sixpence a time. The main feature of the instruction is the tortuous and
incomprehensible language in which the "lesson" is written. Learned and
unnecessary vocabulary is used, obscuring the simple explanation that he
gave to Finbarr; its purpose is to impress the gullible public with the
"Professor's" so-called erudition and to convince buyers that their money
has been well spent. "What's the difference," he asks Finbarr, if you're an
inch or a mile up? "The trick is to put all idea of height out of your
mind" (25). But in the cheaply printed instruction book he sells, long
technical and irrelevant descriptions of the body's balancing mechanism
are set down at length:

The aural labyrinth consists of a number of membranous chambers and tubes
immersed in fluid residing in the cavity of the inner ear, in mammals joined to
the cochlea. The membranous section of the labyrinth consists of two small bags,
the saccule and the utricle, and three semi-circular canals which open into it. The

nerves which supply the labyrinth end with a number of cells attired in hair-like projections which, when grouped, form the two otolith organs in the saccule and utricle and the three *cristae* of the semi-circular canals. In the otolith organs the hair-like protruberances are embedded in a gelatinous mess containing calcium carbonate. (40)

All anatomically correct—and all quite irrelevant to the practicalities of wire walking. The passage is part of O'Brien's satire on pedantry. The brother has learned the value of obfuscation, of surrounding his subject in mystery, and turned it to good financial account—as the collection of sixpenny postal orders in his bedroom drawer testify.

Inevitably, Manus does not stop at this initial success. Working in his "private mine, the National Library" (57), he culls encyclopedias and other works of reference, and turns out such writings as "Swimming and Diving. A Manly and Noble Art" under the name of Lew Paterson, and "Clinical Notes on Pott's Fracture" purporting to be Ernest George Maude. Unlikely though it may seem, these efforts sell.

After Mrs. Crotty's funeral, Manus announces his intention of leaving his uncle's house and establishing himself on Tooley Street, in London, where he has taken out a lease on two rooms. He plans to exchange Dublin's National Library for London's British Museum and to "teach the British to learn French or cure chilblains." When a police sergeant calls to inquire whether Manus was responsible for the course of instruction that induced a child to cross a river on a high wire, nearly drowning in the attempt, Manus disclaims all knowledge of such an enterprise and leaves secretly for England earlier than he planned. Here he establishes himself as the London University Academy, undertaking to offer tuition in subjects as diverse and incongruous as Jujitsu, Political Science, Hypnotism, Astronomy, Woodwork, Care of the Teeth, Cure for Cancer, Treatment of Baldness, Thaumaturgy, The Ancient Classics, and, among many other things, Laundry Management.

His aim, Manus writes to Finbarr, is "the mass-production of knowledge, human accomplishment and civilization . . . not really a Utopia but a society in which all *unnecessary* wrong, failures and misbehaviours are removed" (83). Whether he has convinced himself of this philanthropic turn of mind is not clear, though it is unlikely. Acquisition of wealth with no consideration for his fellow men is Manus's true ruling passion. He acquires a partner in his enterprise—one Milton Byron Barnes—who is keen to launch a major advertising campaign for the academy. Although it is difficult to believe in Manus's censure of

Barnes's greed, Manus reports himself as telling Barnes that "happiness and satisfaction can be achieved by teaching ten thousand Englishmen to play billiards properly." Barnes's answer, Manus says, is that "he doesn't want to make anybody happy and certainly doesn't want to be happy himself; he just wants to make a lot of money" (83). Although Manus only shares these remarks with Finbarr in order to comment that he himself finds such an attitude "a bit cynical," his next sentence suggests that the same motivation drives him: he cultivates Barnes's mother in the hope that she will help the academy "with infusions of the red blood of L.S.D. . . . That is why rich people were made and why we should never envy or insult them."

Manus's letter undoubtedly illustrates his character, but it does have another point of interest. He identifies a general malaise that has been the subject of many modernist and postmodernist writers: "Every day you meet people going around with two heads. They are completely puzzled by life, they understand practically nothing and are certain of only one thing—that they are going to die." Loss of faith and the consequent meaninglessness of life are summed up in those words. The brother has no answer for his diagnosis of twentieth-century alienation: "I am not going to contradict them in that but I believe I can suggest to them a few good ways of filling up the interval" (83).

Whether or not this comment is intended to bring Samuel Beckett to mind is uncertain, but undoubtedly the thought, however differently expressed, is similar to Beckett's. Manus himself is not subject to despair, for it is his intention to make money from other people's emptiness. But his generalization recalls Pozzo's words in *Waiting for Godot:* "They give birth astride of a grave, the light gleams an instant, then it's night once more." Immediately after this remark Pozzo leaves, and Vladimir wakes Estragon, who asks, "Why will you never let me sleep?"

> *Vladimir:* I felt lonely.
> *Estragon:* I was dreaming I was happy.
> *Vladimir:* That passed the time.[5]

O'Brien's exposition is different from Beckett's but the ideas are similar: "They . . . are certain of only one thing—that they are going to die" is like "They give birth astride of a grave"; and Manus and Vladimir are equally aware of the need to "fill up the interval" or "pass the time."

I am not suggesting direct reference to Beckett by O'Brien. It is more interesting to recognize a similar heritage, a similar knowledge of Joyce's work, and the fact that both published their first novels (*At Swim-Two-Birds* and *Murphy*) within a year of each other.

Many reviewers of *The Hard Life* were reminded of Joyce's *Dubliners* and commented on O'Brien's "exegesis of squalor" with Joyce's portrayal of moral squalor and paralysis. O'Brien's use of the word *illumination* in describing *The Hard Life* to his publisher brings to mind Joyce's "epiphanies." It is almost insulting to attempt a comparison between this mediocre production of O'Brien's and the much-earlier *Dubliners* (though both are set in the same decade), but the ending of *The Hard Life* is in that mold. It deliberately fails to resolve any elements of the plot but does imply a moment of self-realization for Finbarr, as well as loathing for his brother and all he stands for.

Manus points out to his brother that, owing to Mr. Collopy's will, Annie is now well provided for. She is also, he says, "an industrious, well-built girl" (125), and he follows up this remark by asking, "Tell me this much: have you ever had a wish for Annie?" Annie has been represented by Finbarr as "a horrible, limp, lank streel of a creature," in spite of his recognition that she has a good heart and works hard (73). But she is also associated in his mind with possible promiscuity and with the possibility of disease that such behavior implies. He also thinks of her only in relation to Penelope, to whom he has lost his heart: "I remember being puzzled that she and Annie belonged to the same sex." Annie, he tells Penelope, "never changes. In fact she never changes even her clothes" (88). And so his response to Manus's suggestion is a horrified "What?" as Manus drains his glass of whiskey and leaves. The novel ends with these words from Finbarr: "The slam of the door told me he was gone. In a daze I lifted my own glass and without knowing what I was doing did exactly what the brother did, drained the glass in one vast swallow. Then I walked quickly but did not run to the lavatory. There everything inside me came up in a tidal surge of vomit." The reference to the whiskey—which Mr. Collopy and Father Fahrt consume throughout, all the while pretending not to be drinkers—works as a culmination of the drinking motif and reverberates, suggesting that Finbarr vomits in response not just to the notion of a liaison with Annie but to his squalid surroundings in general. It is a revolting moment of illumination, epiphany, understanding.

The long, pedantic conversations in which Mr. Collopy and Father Fahrt indulge, coupled with their drinking, also recall the paralysis of Dublin as expressed in Joyce's *Dubliners*. Alcohol and religion are two of the ways in which his Dubliners manage to evade facing up to themselves.

Such parallels may well be incidental, accidental, or unconscious on O'Brien's part. Certainly he was never pleased at comparisons of his work with Joyce's, though it is difficult not to make them.

But in the final paragraph of *The Hard Life* O'Brien may have intentionally referred to the end of Beckett's *Murphy*. Murphy dies by "a classical case of misadventure"[6] but leaves precise instructions for the disposal of his body: it must be cremated and then "placed in a paper bag and brought to the Abbey Theatre, Lr Abbey Street, Dublin, and without pause into what the great and good Lord Chesterfield calls the necessary house, where their happiest hours have been spent, on the right as one goes down into the pit, and I desire that the chain be there pulled upon them, if possible during the performance of a piece."[7] These modest last wishes of the unfortunate Murphy are not carried out. Cooper, who has been charged with the task, gets no further than the bar of a public house, where he throws the paper bag containing Murphy's ashes at a man who has offended him. The bag "bounced, burst, off the wall on to the floor, where it once became the object of much dribbling, passing, tapping, shooting, punching, heading. . . . By closing time the body, mind and soul of Murphy were freely distributed over the floor of the saloon, and before another dayspring greyened the earth had been swept away with the sand, the beer, the butts, the glass, the matches, the spits, the vomit."[8]

Dubliners, Murphy, and *The Hard Life* all describe squalor of one kind or another, but O'Brien's novel fails to reach the achievement of the two earlier works. It has nothing of the intricacy or coherence of Joyce's short story sequence; it is pessimistic, but not in the same way as *Murphy*—it fails entirely to reach Beckett's level of comic seriousness.

The brother is instrumental in the unfortunate death of Mr. Collopy. Finbarr writes to him with details of Collopy's illness, and Manus sends back a long-distance diagnosis of rheumatoid arthritis, together with a bottle of Gravid Water, which, according to him, is a "certain cure." Finbarr conceals its origin from his uncle, who claims to feel better after a week's treatment. But after six weeks, Finbarr notices something strange in the patient's movements: "His walk became most laborious and slow and the floor creaked under him. One night in bed I heard with a start a distant rending crash coming from his bedroom. . . . I hurried down to find him breathless and tangled in the wreckage of his bed" (95). This excuse for sordid detail is not missed: "It seems that the wire mattress, rusted and rotted by Mrs. Crotty's nocturnal diureses (or bed-wetting) had collapsed under Mr. Collopy's weight" (96).

Weight is the important factor. Mr. Collopy now weighs 29 stone (406 pounds), although his actual physical shape is unaltered. Manus elucidates the mystery: owing to a misunderstanding of the directions on the bottle—"t/spoon"—Finbarr has been administering tablespoons, not teaspoons, of Gravid Water. The Gravid Water Finbarr tells us "was calculated to bring about a gradual and controlled increase in weight and thus to cause a redevelopment of the rheumatoid joints by reason of the superior weight and the increased work they would have to do" (97). Without declaring this state of affairs to Mr. Collopy, Manus decides to send him and Father Fahrt on a pilgrimage to Rome: "I do not think it is in the least presumptuous to expect a miracle and have Mr. Collopy restored to his proper weight." The reason for the pilgrimage is not disclosed to the pilgrims—who remain unaware of Manus's involvement with Mr. Collopy's ill health.

Finbarr remains in Dublin and hears of the ill-fated trip only through his brother's letters, which form the main part of the narrative toward the end of the novel. Manus organizes an audience with the pope, the outcome of which is disastrous.

The Pope:	How do things fare in your country, beloved Ireland?
Collopy:	Only middling, Your Holiness. The British are still there.
The Pope:	And is the country not prosperous?
Collopy:	I do not think so, Your Holiness, for there is much unemployment in Dublin. (109)

So far, so good. But Mr. Collopy is not content, and urges (though it is still not stated openly) his petition for public conveniences for women. The pope pronounces that Collopy suffers from serious delusions and obsessions, asserts that Father Fahrt is culpable in encouraging him, and concludes that it is unseemly to consult the latter on such matters. The pilgrims are dismissed. Manus's next letter informs Finbarr of Collopy's untimely death: his weight was too great for a wooden landing at the top of some stairs and he dies after the fall. O'Brien exploits the grotesqueness of the situation to the full: "There was apparently no access to the space under the stairs and two carpenters using hatchets, saws and chisels were carefully breaking down the woodwork in the hallway below the landing" (116). Manus remains, as always, emotionally detached from the proceedings and appears to have no conscience about his part in his uncle's death. He merely reports that he was interested in the rapid decomposition of the body; though he is not certain, he hazards a guess that "here was the Gravid Water again." He does, however, change the label on the bottle to guard against future overdoses.

The whole episode reads rather like an excuse for a Myles na gCopaleen "Keats and Chapman" pun from O'Brien's *Irish Times* column, and indeed Keats has his part to play. Manus chooses for Collopy's epitaph a variation on Keats's own: "Here lies one whose name is writ on water" becomes, for Collopy, "Here lies one whose name is writ *in* water" (121; my italics). Rather a lot of labor for so slender a satisfaction!

The only comeuppance Manus receives is to find himself excluded from Collopy's will: he left £500 to each of the boys on the condition that both were still resident in his house at the time of his death.

O'Brien was confident of his achievement in *The Hard Life*. He wrote to Mark Hamilton (who worked for his agent), "It may sound rash and silly to say so but I am convinced that this book will be a resounding success, though possibly after a slow start. The greatest living European arbiter of literature said first that the book paralysed him and finally confessed it was 'a gem.' I mean Brendan Behan."[9]

In November 1961 after publication, he described to Timothy O'Keeffe the reactions of two people who had not heard of the book before he gave them copies: "The first found it very, very funny— uproarious. The second (a lady) handed it back to me sadly. She said she did not understand me and now doubted whether she ever had. But of one thing I could be sure. Not one night would pass but she would say a Hail Mary for me. And wasn't it a good job my poor mother wasn't still alive?"[10] The woman had been particularly shocked by the name of the Jesuit father, Fahrt. O'Brien had chosen this name deliberately because of its coarse Anglo-Saxon meaning. It certainly reiterates the schoolboy lavatory humor that passes for comedy in the book, and O'Brien's intention was to shock: "That was exactly what I thought would happen. That name will cause holy bloody ructions here."[11] Against his hopes the book did not achieve fame by being banned, and ructions did not take place—though not for want of trying on O'Brien's part. He suggested to the publishers that instead of his photograph appearing on the cover, "the back could carry a picture of a head (anybody's—Martin Luther's?) with the slogan ST. THOMAS AQUINAS WOULD HAVE LIKED THIS BOOK, FOR HE WROTE—and here would follow a piece of bullshit written by me (with occasional Latin glosses). This would amuse the sophisticates, impress the ignoramuses, and drive the Jesuits mad with anger."[12] The publishers, probably quite wisely, decided against adopting these suggestions.

O'Brien was not the best judge of his own work. In spite of some good reviews—Simon Raven in the *Spectator* called the book a "memorable essay in black comedy,"[13] for example—O'Brien's confidence in *The Hard Life* was mistaken, and it is unlikely that the work would remain in print today were it not of interest purely because it came from the author of *At Swim-Two-Birds, The Third Policeman,* and *The Poor Mouth.*

Chapter Six

The Dalkey Archive

O'Brien started writing *The Dalkey Archive* in 1962.[1] Typically, it is a work that emphasizes a number of ideas at the expense of characterization, or psychological depth, aspects we often expect to find in a novel. But it is certainly "novel" in the word's original sense of "a novelty." In a letter to Timothy O'Keeffe, O'Brien outlined the ideas behind the book, beginning with the concept of time that allows him to introduce into his fiction, as characters, historical figures as diverse as Saint Augustine and James Joyce. "The idea," he wrote, "is that time is as a great flat motionless sea. Time does not pass; it is we who pass. With this concept as basic, fantastic but coherent situations can easily be devised, and in effect the whole universe torn up in a monstrous comic debauch. Such obsessions as nuclear energy, space travel and landing men on the moon can be made to look as childish and insignificant as they probably are. Anything can be brought in, including the long-overdue rehabilitation of Judas Iscariot."[2]

That the "ideas" rather than the storytelling were uppermost in O'Brien's mind is apparent from another comment in the same letter: "There is a pedestrian sub-theme that keeps the major concept in order as in a vice." The subtheme concerns Mick Shaughnessy, his girlfriend Mary, and his friend Hackett, who all live in Dalkey, a small town to the south of Dublin.

O'Brien is, as usual, concerned with the fantastic as well as the comic. We do not have to believe in the fiction, but by anchoring the extraordinary to the prosaic, O'Brien does not overstretch our credulity or our disbelief. The other side of this coin, one he also used to great effect in *The Third Policeman,* is that of making what we think of as reality—the ordinary world we inhabit—rather more uncomfortable and unfamiliar than we are accustomed to. As usual, his fiction borders on the surreal; he was concerned that "some stupid critic (and which of them is not?)" would praise him as "a master of science fiction"[3]—which is not how he intended the work to be read.

The story is straightforward. Mick and Hackett meet a physicist called

96

De Selby (a name he had used in *The Third Policeman*), who tells them of his plans to exterminate mankind on the grounds that the human race merits destruction. "Its history and pre-history, even its present, is a foul record of pestilence, famine, war, devastation and misery so terrible and multifarious that its depth and horror are unknown to any one man. Rottenness is universally endemic, disease is paramount. The human race is finally debauched and aborted" (18). The substance De Selby has invented—D.M.P.—is capable of extracting all oxygen from the atmosphere. Mick appoints himself savior of mankind and, with the local policeman's help, steals the substance. In the intervening time, De Selby has introduced Mick and Hackett to Saint Augustine; Mick has discovered that James Joyce, though old, is alive and living in Skerries; and that (as in *The Third Policeman*) people are turning into bicycles and vice versa.

In his letter to O'Keeffe O'Brien mentioned J. W. Dunne's book *An Experiment with Time* (1927) as an important influence in his initial conception of *The Dalkey Archive*. While it is not necessary to follow all of Dunne's arguments in order to understand O'Brien's fantasy, *An Experiment with Time* is an interesting link between physics, literature, and the theological questions that O'Brien raises—and inevitably fails to answer. The handling of time is fundamental to all novelists and novels. The philosopher Henri Bergson's theories seem to have had direct application to writers like Proust, Joyce, and Woolf, all of whom expressed in their fiction an awareness of the difference between external (or clock) time and a different inner sense of duration. These ideas are fundamental to the modernist development of interior monologue. Einstein's theory of relativity was important too. On the subject of Einstein and the relativists, Dunne says: "They exactly reversed the procedures of the nineteenth-century Time dimensionalists. . . . Einstein [enunciated] for the first time in history, not merely that different individuals could hold different views regarding both Time (as measured by clocks) and Space (as measured by rods) but that such judgements could be equally valid."[4] Dunne himself went further, suggesting that although we commonly think of time in terms of length, there is no such thing as the passage of time; instead, all time is eternally present. In his opinion we age independently from time—growing older is simply a manifestation of organic decay. In *The Dalkey Archive* Saint Augustine tells De Selby that "your sort of time is merely a confusing index of decomposition" (34).

In practice, *The Dalkey Archive* does not owe a great deal to such

details, though when De Selby asks Saint Augustine what it feels like to
be in heaven for "all eternity," the saint replies, "For *all* eternity? Do you
think there are fractional or temporary eternities?" When asked if he will
consent to return tomorrow, Augustine says, "I have no tomorrow. I am. I
have only nowness" (43). Again, a number of technical scientific questions are addressed when De Selby explains to Mick and Hackett what
they must do in order to observe and overhear his conversation with Saint
Augustine. They are to swim to an underwater cave, which is totally
sealed by water at high tide: "We get to the empty chamber . . . and I
then release a minute quantity of D.M.P. We are then subsisting in
timeless nitrogen but still able to breathe from the tanks on our backs"
(24). De Selby provides them with oxygen tanks: "The air is compressed
and will last half an hour by conventional effluxion of time" (31). These
tanks are vital because terrestial atmosphere, as well as the "time
illusion," is annihilated by activating the D.M.P. O'Brien, though
fascinated by problems of physics, sidesteps any shortcomings in his
scientific explanations, and disarms readers by allowing De Selby to ask
the two young men whether everything is clear: "I don't want any
attempt at technical guff or questions at this time" (31). The novelist
surfaces and the scientist retreats, as indeed, given that his business is
fiction, he has every right to do.

There is a point at which literature and physics are closely bound: both
attempt to describe the world we live in. Rather than continuing to trace
specific influences of Dunne's work on O'Brien's fiction, it is more
appropriate to ask a broader question: if science can provide no certain
physical laws for the universe, how can literature present us with anything
other than uncertainties? The question is not just one of concepts; it
concerns the more fundamental problem of language. For example,
Dunne imagines trying to describe the color red to a blind man: "You
might talk to him of particles (lumps—centres of inertia), and describe
these as oscillating, spinning, circling, colliding, and rebounding in any
kind of complicated dance you cared to imagine. But in all that there
would be nothing to introduce the notion of *redness.*"[5] "Redness," he goes
on to say, "may not be a thing—but it is very certainly a *fact . . . and the
language of physics is fundamentally unadapted to the task of rendering
that account.*"[6] It is not simply the language of physics but language in
general that is inadequate to the task of providing anything other
than an approximation to the world it seeks to describe. Undoubtedly it is the best form of communication we have, but words only
represent things, objects, activities, or emotions; they are not those

things themselves. Words do not exactly reproduce that to which they refer.

When O'Brien introduces Saint Augustine into his novel, naturally enough the plot requires that De Selby question him about eternity. On this subject, however, O'Brien the novelist is in no better position to answer than any of his readers. Using his authorial license to deflect criticism, he has De Selby express dissatisfaction with the saint's answers. Augustine responds by saying, "Discourse must be in words, and it is not possible to give a name to that which is not understood nor cogniscible by human reason" (41). "Discourse must be in words," and O'Brien was aware that they are an imperfect medium.

Some years later, Hugh Leonard was engaged in dramatizing *The Dalkey Archive* for stage performance. O'Brien wrote him a word of warning: "You must remember that the most crackpot invention must be subject to its own stern logic."[7] O'Brien could have "conjured" Saint Augustine into his novel without adverting to physics at all, but physical laws become something of a theme in the book, as O'Brien incorporated material into it from the rejected manuscript of *The Third Policeman*. Sergeant Fottrell explains to Mick that the well-documented fact that molecules of iron are transferred from hammer to anvil and anvil to hammer on impact is actually operating in a wider and more sinister way with cyclists and their bicycles—owing to rough riding over badly kept roads. The sergeant is obliged never to mount his bike, always to push it, and to steal regularly the bicycles of habitual cyclists in order to save them from this terrible fate. The implications are that the familiar world is in fact virtually unknowable, that we pretend to understand it because doing so is more comfortable than confronting its unfathomable mysteries.

As Mick sits in the public house with the sergeant's revelations running fresh through his mind, he thinks of one particular country scene:

Brown bogs and black bogs were arranged neatly on each side of the road with rectangular boxes carved out of them here and there, each with a filling of yellow-brown brown-yellow water. Far away near the sky tiny people were stooped at their turf-work, cutting out precisely-shaped sods with their patent spades and building them into a tall memorial twice the height of a horse and cart. Sounds came from them, delivered to his ears without charge by the west wind, sounds of laughing and whistling and bits of verses from the old bog songs. Nearer, a house stood attended by three trees. . . . The house was quiet in itself and silent but a canopy of lazy smoke had been erected over the chimney to indicate that people were within engaged on tasks. Ahead of him went the road,

running swiftly across the flat land and pausing slightly to climb slowly up a hill
that was waiting for it in a place where there was tall grass, grey boulders and
rank stunted trees. The whole overhead was occupied by the sky, translucent,
impenetrable, ineffable and incomparable, with a fine island of cloud anchored in
the calm two yards to the right of Mr. Jarvis's outhouse. (82–83)

This passage was taken from its original context in the *Third Policeman*
(74), the only difference being that there it is written in the first person.
The same passage serves entirely different purposes in each novel,
however. In *The Third Policeman* the representation of reality has to be
slightly ambiguous, because when we reread, we realize that it is not our
world that is being described, but hell. In *The Dalkey Archive,* ironically,
the passage represents a touchstone of reality for Mick when his ideas and
knowledge of the universe are shaken. The scene is typical of O'Brien's
descriptive writing, but if it is "real" and "incontrovertible" on the page
of the book, those are the last things it is in comparison with traditional
realistic writing. The whole passage exudes a sense of composition, not
least in the use of such words as *neatly arranged* and *erected;* it reads like a
description of a painted or stage-flat landscape. Perspectives are misleading, and so the "tiny people" are not near the horizon but "near the
sky"; Mick can see that the sods of turf they cut are "precisely shaped"
with—even closer detail—"patent spades." The passage gains its disturbing qualities not so much from the narrative turn of phrase as from a
sense of an unknown arranging hand at work, *designing* the landscape.
Familiar objects are presented in such a way that unease and a sense of
*un*familiarity are generated. It is so two-dimensionally concrete that what
we may initially accept as conventional realism is actually, on closer
examination, about to topple over into pure fantasy. If one's visual
imagination constructs to the letter what one reads, then the impression
received is one of unnaturalness. It assumes connotations of Dunne's
feeling: "The universe begins to look more like a great thought than a
great machine."[8] The world is a difficult and unknowable place—more
frightening and incomprehensible here than in *The Third Policeman,*
where we can ultimately "account" for it as taking place in hell. That
there are "more things in heaven and earth than are dreamed of in your
philosophy" is an unspoken gesture toward *Hamlet* in a text that alludes
to that play more than once.

   O'Brien dedicated *The Dalkey Archive* to "my Guardian Angel,
impressing upon him that I'm only fooling and warning him to see to it
that there is no misunderstanding when I go home." In itself this

statement is amusing, but it may also have been the result of more serious
worries. O'Brien suffered from ill health and bizarre accidents while
working on the book. He wrote an article for the *Guardian* blaming all
these woes on Saint Augustine, claiming that Augustine was "getting his
own back" for O'Brien's portrayal of him in the novel. The last quarter of
The Dalkey Archive was written "in hospital under appalling conditions
(some of it under an anaesthetic, I suspect)," he wrote to Cecil Scott.[9]
O'Brien was involved in a car crash in October 1963 and suffered a
fractured and dislocated shoulder and a badly broken leg, as well as
"trivialities" like concussion and a "bashed-in face." In April of the
following year he wrote to Cecil Scott about another accident:

The main injury was a shattered right leg. My Irish surgeon while removing
hip-to-toe plaster confided to me that he was suffering severely from influenza.
When I got home I found the leg was completely paralyzed as if cast in concrete,
without the slightest motion possible at the knee or ankle joints: in other words,
the muscles are completely atrophied. There is apparently nothing to do for
several weeks but sit in a chair and make excruciating attempts to get movement
back, groaning softly the while. As I think I said before, I blame it all on
Augustine.[10]

But he was interested in Saint Augustine and went to great lengths of
research in the interest of accuracy: "Augustine is a wonderful man, if he
ever existed. Probably the most abandoned young man of his day,
immersed in thievery and graft and determined to get up on every woman
or girl he meets, he reaches a point of satiation and meekly turns to
bestiality and buggery. (His Confessions are the dirtiest book on earth.)
When he had become saintly, he was a terrible blister in the side of
organized Christianity because he angrily held (and he was one of the
Fathers of the Church) that there was no such place as Purgatory."[11]
   Some of the people who read the manuscript were uncertain about the
Augustine scenes, but O'Brien defended them on the grounds that he
thought them funny, and that the material he was presenting was serious
and accurate.

I believe I have read everything about Augustine published in English, French,
German and Latin and, though an inept result could not be defended by saying
that hard work preceded it, I believe the chapter is a fair exposition of St.
Augustine as he appears to the independent mind today. Nobody can be certain
whether he was a genuine holy man or a humbug, headcase. In my research I

soon found that no reliance whatever was to be placed on the commonly available works of Augustine in translation (mostly by clerics) to English or French: it was the rule to dilate or deliberately mistranslate many of his robust and brave avowals and confessions.[12]

In the novel most of the comedy comes from Augustine's unexpected Dublin idiom. His first words, in response to De Selby's thanks for his appearance, are "Ah not at all man" (34), and he accounts for debauchery in his youth as "the Irish in me. . . . My father's name was Patrick. And he was a proper gobshite." The incongruity of his language—"Two Saint Patricks? We have *four* of the buggers in our place and they'd make you sick with their shamrocks and shenanigans and bullshit"—is the other main source of humor. The saint is cantankerous and holds his fellow inhabitants of heaven in scant reverence: Saint Peter, for instance, is "just out to show off the keys, bluster about and make himself a bloody nuisance" (37). Significantly, Augustine's Irishness is not such a feature toward the end of his dialogue with De Selby. He is questioned about free will (something Dunne addressed in *An Experiment with Time*) and about what happened to all the "souls" who died before Christ was crucified. Augustine's reply is serious: "If you would know God, you must know time. God is time. God is the substance of eternity. God is not distinct from what we regard as years. God has no past, no future, no presence in the sense of man's fugitive tenure. The interval you mention between the Creation and the Redemption was ineffably unexistent" (42).

Neither Mick nor Hackett is aware until afterward that it is Augustine whom they have seen and heard. Hackett makes a lighthearted remark—"I thought it was Santa Claus"—but his voice has lost its usual jeering quality (44). De Selby issues a word of warning, however, and asks them to remember that it may not have been the genuine Augustine at all:

—But who then?
The wise master stared out to sea. It could be even Beelzebub himself, he murmured softly. (45)

The implications are not quite so serious, for neither Mick nor Hackett is obliged to act in any way following the ghostly manifestation. Yet the parallels with Hamlet, uncertain whether his supernatural visitation was actually his father or a diabolic spirit, underlie the surface of the text.

O'Brien does not have to resort to the machinations of D.M.P. in order to introduce James Joyce into his novel. Mick chats to Dr. Crewett in the Colza Hotel and mentions Joyce in passing: "Consider the wonderful reputation won by the late James Joyce." Dr. Crewett puts down his glass and asks what Mick means by "the late James Joyce."

—I thought everybody knew that Joyce's death—all those reports in foreign newspapers in the confusion of war—was all my eye.
—You mean that Joyce is still alive?
—Certainly I do.
—Then why didn't he contradict the reports? Such unfounded reports could be actionable.
—Because he put the story out himself. (98)

Mick determines to discover Joyce's whereabouts, partly to gain Mary's admiration. He tells Dr. Crewett that he is merely curious, because he admires Joyce's dexterity and resource in handling language, his accuracy of dialogue, and his sense of humor. But he adds that he has read some of the "stupid books written *about* Joyce" (103) and suggests that a "real" book about him, based on long conversations, could clear up mistakes and "eliminate a lot of stupidity" (104).

"It is quite true," O'Brien wrote to Cecil Scott, "that James Joyce has been dragged in by the scruff of his neck but I think this is quite permissible within the spoofy canon of the book. . . . The intention here is not to make Joyce himself ridiculous but to say something funny about the preposterous image of him that emerges from the treatment he has received at the hands of many commentators and exegetists (mostly, alas, American)."[13]

It was the critical industry that had already flourished on Joyce's work by the early 1960s that irritated O'Brien. His fictional portrayal is one that firmly reduces Joyce's elevated status and makes him appear not only human but homely. O'Brien's Joyce refuses to acknowledge authorship of *Ulysses* and knows nothing of the existence of *Finnegans Wake*. There can be no greater refutation of Joyce than to have him condemn his own masterpiece as "a dirty boring subject" (185).

When Mick finally tracks Joyce down, he is working behind a bar in Skerries. Mick, thinking of *A Portrait of the Artist as a Young Man* and Stephen's renunciation of not only his family and country but also his faith, is shocked when Joyce enlists his help in his desire to join the Jesuits. When an introduction to Father Cobble is finally effected, it is Mick's embarrassment that registers when the father offers

Joyce work mending the Jesuits' underclothes. Mick's final thought is to ask himself whether he had "cynically made a fool of Joyce," though he concludes that if that was the result, it was not his intention (196).

At his first meeting with Joyce, Mick asks if he has any new work on hand: "Writing is not quite the word," Joyce replies, "assembly, perhaps, is better—or accretion" (133). This description is accurate for *Finnegans Wake* and, incidentally, would apply in a different sense to *At Swim-Two-Birds*. But it is not the *Wake* that Joyce has in mind: he emerges instead as someone who has written tracts for the Catholic Truth Society of Ireland and published a biographical piece on Saint Cyril, Apostle of the Slavs, for the Irish Jesuit quarterly (175). O'Brien's Joyce has certainly heard of *Ulysses* but claims it was the result of Sylvia Beach's infatuation with him: "[H]er plot was to have this thing named *Ulysses* concocted, secretly circulated and have the authorship ascribed to me" (176). Mick, still unconvinced about the accuracy of this information or the reliability of Joyce's memory, tells Joyce that the book is a work to be proud of. "Well, well, well," Joyce comments, "I am going out for a moment to relieve myself. I feel that's about the perfect thing to do" (178). He is referring to the climax of *Ulysses,* which comes in the penultimate chapter. Stephen Dedalus has met Bloom, and after cocoa and conversation in Bloom's kitchen, the two men urinate together under the night sky in Bloom's garden. The metaphor is one of the "waters of life"—their friendship will not develop, but both have been given new impetus by meeting and talking. By including this offhand allusion, O'Brien demonstrates his own knowledge and understanding of Joyce's work—a tribute for which Joyce would probably have forgiven him his wickedly comic distortion of his life's work and beliefs.

Mick's plan for introducing Joyce to De Selby comes to nothing, but his projection of a meeting between the two is momentous in its implications: Mick "resolved by bringing together De Selby and Joyce and inducing them both to devote their considerable brains in consultation to some recondite, involuted and incomprehensible literary project, ending in publication of a book which would be commonly ignored and thus be no menace to universal sanity" (116).

Although he said that Joyce had been "dragged in by the scruff of his neck," O'Brien actually prepared for Joyce's entrance on the first page of *The Dalkey Archive* by alluding to the Italian philosopher Giambattista Vico. Joyce's use of Vico's belief that history runs in recurring cycles was well documented; it is fundamental to the cyclical structure of *Finnegans*

Wake. O'Brien seized on the fact that the Vico Road is an actual topographical feature—the road to Dalkey, and the way in which readers approach the place in O'Brien's novel. Why the road was so named is unknown, but O'Brien makes good use of it. His narrator asks, "Why this name Vico Road? Is there to be recalled in this magnificence a certain philosopher's lot on earth—thesis, antithesis, synthesis, chaos?" (7). "Hardly," he concludes, yet he has clearly expressed Vico's notion of history in that sentence—though the philosophical use, later in the novel, of Dunne's ideas about time would probably refute Vico's views. The narrator refers to the place of Vico's birth, wondering whether the Vico Road was "to be compared with the Bay of Naples." Again, he thinks not—the Irish climate is softer. O'Brien has not referred to Joyce by name, but the allusion is there to prepare any informed reader.

The Dalkey Archive is the only one of O'Brien's novels to be written in the third person. The earliest draft was a first-person narrative, with Mick himself telling the story, but the desire to portray Mick as more objectionable made O'Brien revise the work. "I showed the MS to a friend whose opinion I value very much," he wrote to Cecil Scott, "and was very pleased when he suggested, among other things, a major change which I had already decided on without his knowledge: that is, the obliteration of the first person sing. narrator. This character is a conceited prig and a change to the third person would materially change, so to speak, the camera angle, and facilitate the job of making him more revolting."[14] O'Brien put this matter more cryptically when he wrote to Mark Hamilton some weeks later: "A fundamental reform is the annihilation of the first person singular as narrator; this character must not only become a more obnoxious pest than at present but also third person singular and very third class."[15] The third-person narrative is an objective one, but it does follow Mick's point of view; we have no interior views of the other characters' thoughts. And in any event, Mick is not unduly toadlike. His most outstanding characteristic is his ordinariness; even his developing pretensions are an understandable consequence of this quality.

Like O'Brien himself, Mick is employed as a civil servant—in popular imagination a mundane and pedestrian occupation. It is a nice irony, however, for his belief that he is to perform a service to civilization—by ridding the world of D.M.P.—gives him delusions of grandeur. After witnessing De Selby's powers and forming plans to defeat them with Sergeant Foterill's help, he believes "that his own function and standing had risen remarkably. He was *supervising* men of indeterminate calibre, or sanity that was more than suspect. Clearly enough this task had been assigned to him by Almighty God, and this gave him the status of priest. He was certainly as much a priest as Father Cobble, whom both De Selby and himself had dismissed as stupid" (143). In chapter 17, he has assumed what he thinks of as even more responsibility—in terms of state now, as well as religion: "[T]he cares on him were heavy, and somehow he seemed to be taking on the character of a Cabinet Minister. What did he mean Cabinet Minister? Prime Minister was the more precise term. Policy in several major regards was in his sole charge; he was making—and had made—critical decisions" (170).

In keeping with his new self-imposed status, Mick decides to enter an enclosed religious order once he has finished dealing with these major problems; he forswears boozing in favor of mineral water (and almost succeeds) and determines to relinquish his fiancée, Mary, in favor of his higher calling. None of these good resolutions come to anything; his plans for lending a helping hand to James Joyce also fail. But undoubtedly he thinks of himself as a savior: "In all his muddling supernatural and scientific diversions, Mick reminded himself, he must not lose sight of that true manifestation of humanity's nobility—*compassion*. Beside it any other virtue was shallow and poor" (150).

He lends a financially embarrassed friend £3 and asks himself afterward, as he sits down to black coffee and buns," Was it not the sort of repast . . . which behoved the Good Samaritan?" (151). The narrative is ironic at his expense. When Mick goes into the Colza Hotel in the last chapter, Hackett underlines Mick's romantic image of himself with heavy sarcasm: "Enter the Prince of Denmark!" (199). A less heroic figure than Mick would be hard to find.

Mick's decision to tell Mary that he has no further time for her, because of his intention to join the Trappists, never passes his lips; his interest in her is rearoused as soon as Hackett declares that he is going to marry her. "One thing about Mary," Hackett says, with a perception we have not noted in his character before, "she's alive. You never suspected that or if you did, you kept the discovery secret" (201). But Mick and Mary are soon reconciled, and the novel ends with plans for their marriage and "little house." The last words of the novel introduce an element of disturbing comic ambiguity, however.

—It's an old fashioned idea, [Mary says,] but a roof means security—for ourselves and the family.

–The family?
–Yes, Mick. I'm certain I'm going to have a baby.

No explanation follows, and the reader, like Mick, presumably, is left bewildered. Is Mary merely speaking with confidence of the future, or is she actually pregnant now? She has been dancing, drinking, and going out to shows with Hackett over the past few weeks while Mick has been preoccupied; if she is expecting a baby, is Hackett, then, the father? or is Mick? More disturbingly, given that her name is Mary, is this situation a continuation of the mysteries of theology that run through the book? Are we to infer that while Mick has seen himself as in some way "chosen," Mary has been singled out by divine intervention for the honor of immaculate conception? By ending the novel in this way, O'Brien poses a question that, for example, Stephen Dedalus wrestled with in *A Portrait of the Artist*: are women whores or Madonnas? Of course they are neither. If you are a man, you might be lucky enough to find a woman who is both, but throughout the ages images in art and literature—particularly of a religious turn—have shown women as either temptresses or objects for adoration intended to lift a man's thoughts to more spiritual planes.

In response to Cecil Scott's criticism, O'Brien wrote, "Yes, Mary is . . . unsatisfactory, though she had not been intended as very much more than a 'fringe benefit' " (6 January 1964). Nevertheless, she is much the most attractive and dwelt on of all O'Brien's female characters. There are few women in his novels. When he was asked about this issue by a BBC interviewer, O'Brien replied, "Well, women are not important in Ireland in any sense of the social determinance, if there's such a word. . . . What I mean is they make our breakfast and they make our beds, but they are not really formative. . . . [T]hey're not really a social force in this country. . . . [Y]ou can't leave them out but you mustn't allow them to intrude too much. It would be a very artificial book that gave women a big role."[16]

While few women could read such opinions today without feeling their hackles rise, it is true that the kind of social life O'Brien lived— consisting almost entirely of meeting other men and drinking in bars—would naturally exclude women, who, according to O'Brien, were not catered for in public houses because lavatories were not provided. This lack of public conveniences for women forms part of the subplot of *The Hard Life*. Undoubtedly O'Brien was devoted to his mother, and presumably to his wife too, but they belonged to his private life and

certainly do not figure in his fiction. As Mary says in *The Dalkey Archive,*
the book O'Brien was planning when he gave the interview just quoted,
"One must write outside oneself" (203). Significantly enough, this belief,
which O'Brien himself held, is here put into a woman's mouth.

Mothers are usually absent in O'Brien's fiction, as in *At Swim-Two-
Birds,* or die while their offspring are young, as in *The Third Policeman* and
The Hard Life. With the exception of Bonaparte in *The Poor Mouth,* none
of O'Brien's protagonists marry—and Bonaparte's mother and wife are
present more as a condition of the writing O'Brien was parodying than as
characters in their own right. Mary is thus unusual, and until the moment
of doubt is cast on her morality at the very end, she is very attractive. She
is an independent, intelligent, educated young woman. Mary, Mick
thinks, is "a superb lady" (61). "She was an unusual girl. She was
educated with a year in France, and understood music. She had wit, could
be lively, and it took little to induce for a while gaiety of word and
mood. . . . She was tasteful and fastidious in dress . . . and why not? She
worked in what was called a fashion house, with a top job which Mick
knew paid well and involved consorting only with people of standing.
. . . She read a lot, talked politics often and once even mentioned her
half-intention of writing a book" (55–56).

High praise indeed. It is Mick's perception of her, not Mary herself,
that becomes disenchanted as the novel progresses. As Mick becomes
more self-important he begins to doubt her and to resent her influence
over him—we have no interior views of Mary's thoughts to corroborate
this point, but we do see quite clearly that Mick becomes more priggish
and unlikable: "First, Mary was indefatigable in probing and catechizing
him, even in matters which were strikingly his own business. She was very
careful to underline her own independence from him as a male escort and
was quite unrestrained in expressing her own ideas on art, manners,
customs, even politics" (141–42). Qualities Mick previously considered
to be virtues become the opposite when he decides Mary is merely a
distraction from his important mission: "Probably she could manage
brief quotes from Mallarmé or Voltaire when the feat seemed opportune.
A reasonable case could be made for establishing that in fact she despised
him. What was she, really, but a gilded trollop, probably with plenty of
other gents who were devout associates. Or slaves, marionettes?" (142). If
O'Brien intended to make Mick toadlike, then this is the point at which
the character demonstrates that quality most clearly. Mick convinces
himself that Mary is shallow and superficial with no real reference to his
actual experience of her.

In many ways, though, Mary is an "unsatisfactory" character. She is certainly the most sustained and pleasant of O'Brien's female characters, but she is not really dramatized in the novel. We note and approve her common sense in response to Mick's preposterous tale about meeting Saint Augustine, but otherwise we are merely *told* by the narrative that she has attractive qualities, and we are obliged to take them on trust. On the other hand, had we been *shown* that she was undoubtedly made of sterling stuff, the ambiguity at the end of the novel would lose its impact. We have Mick's estimation that she is "superb," followed by his disenchantment: she might be a "trollop." Without these diametrically opposed views there would be no dramatization of the well brought up Roman Catholic young man's dilemma at the end—a second Virgin Mary, or not?

Mick lives with his mother, an arrangement that again is unusual for one of O'Brien's protagonists. Mrs. Shaughnessy does not feature largely in the work, but Mick does consider her, and it seems strange that in this most "ideas" based novel, O'Brien has moments that are touching in their humanity. Such moments in a book by another novelist would probably pass unnoticed, but in O'Brien's work they draw attention to themselves by their very rarity. Mick considers that

it might be thought odd that his poor mother, with whom he lived alone, so little occupied his thoughts. She was simple and devout. . . . She was indeed an old woman and to talk to her even in the mildest and most superficial way about De Selby was unthinkable. . . . If she understood a word, she would charitably conclude that he had "a sup taken," for, having loved his father and accepted that he died from drink, she well knew he was no stranger to the taverns. Yes, it is strange and sad to live so close to one so dear and yet have no real point of contact outside banal and trivial smalltalk. (64)

This passage is not mere sentiment but, rather, genuine recognition that experience can separate us from those otherwise close to us. It would be misguided to attempt to wrench biographical significance from these words—O'Brien's father was not, so far as is recorded, a hard-drinking man. But the passage is interesting because it acknowledges affection, a quality peculiarly absent from the bulk of O'Brien's work.

Chapter Seven
Slattery's Sago Saga
and Other Writing

O'Brien completed seven chapters of *Slattery's Sago Saga*[1] before he died, and although that is a fairly substantial amount of material, it is not possible to tell how the story would have developed or what its structure would have been had O'Brien finished the work. It bears many of the hallmarks of his other fiction, as well as some surprises. Like *The Hard Life* and *The Dalkey Archive*, *Slattery's Sago Saga* is a linear, chronological narrative. References to President Kennedy place it firmly in the 1960s, and the fact that one of the characters, Ned Hoolihan, is living in Texas, making more money than he knows what to do with, expands the horizons of the book in a way O'Brien had not previously attempted. O'Brien intended to set some of the action in the United States but never reached that stage of the story. Ned's letter home, however—a document that takes up the whole of the seventh chapter—provides ample opportunity for a description of the American way of life as it appears to an expatriate Irishman. O'Brien had visited America on several occasions, though Ned's account in the book owes more to imagination and popular conception than to any firsthand experience of his creator's.

Tim Hartigan is in charge of Ned's affairs in Ireland. As is the case with all O'Brien protagonists, Tim's parentage is shrouded in mystery: he did have a mother—briefly—but no father. Left "an orphan at the age of two by his widowed mother," he was adopted by Ned Hoolihan, a wealthy man before he left Ireland, a man who had simply "taken a fancy to him" (24). The novel opens when Tim's status quo is disturbed by a letter from Ned telling him to expect the arrival of one Crawford MacPherson. This person is not the "bleeding Scotchman" that Tim anticipates, but the most dynamic female character O'Brien ever created, a woman who, in spite of her Scottish Presbyterian background, converted to Roman Catholicism in order to marry, sort out, and protect Ned Hoolihan and his interests. For a character dating from that period and from O'Brien's pen in particular, Crawford is extraordinarily independent. She is a whiskey-drinking, hard-talking woman, the likes of whom had never before appeared in his fiction. She is, moreover, a woman with a mission. According to Crawford, the biggest tragedy of the Irish potato famine in the preceding century was not death by starvation but the fact that "over a million of those starving Irish tinkers escaped to my adopted country, the United States. . . . They very nearly ruined America. They bred and multiplied and infested the whole continent, saturating it with crime, drunkenness, illegal corn liquor, bank robbery, murder, prostitution, syphilis, mob rule, crooked politics and Roman Catholic Popery" (33).

The list, characteristic of O'Brien's style from his earliest writing, continues: "adultery, salacious dancing, blackmail, drug peddling, pimping, organising brothels, consorting with niggers and getting absolution for all their crimes from Roman Catholic priests." Such crimes are reminiscent of those Trellis was charged with in *At Swim-Two-Birds*—and are as preposterous. Crawford is undoubtedly a tartar, but she is also appreciative when work is carried out efficiently or with understanding. She is the only female character O'Brien ever created who has real vitality.

Other aspects of Crawford, her sex apart, are more familiar. Her plans to change the pattern of nature and society recall the mad scientist De Selby in *The Dalkey Archive*. And although her motives are to alleviate human suffering—"[T]he money at my disposal must be applied to the amelioration of man's lot in general" (68)—the amount of disturbance and devastation her plans would cause if carried out would undoubtedly have featured in the overall plan of the book.

The planting of sago trees and the ban on growing potatoes in Ireland are worthy of O'Brien's imagination at its most fantastic; typically, they are rooted in painstaking research and carried through with a seeming logic that, as usual, borders on the surreal. But if his imagination was fertile, his execution failed in the attempt. An experimental novel like *At Swim* could incorporate pedantic passages of information and not only survive but elicit admiration for sheer audacity. This is not the case with the more conventional narrative that *Slattery's Sago Saga* was destined to be. Chapter 5 consists of two short paragraphs that establish Tim in a library, and then five (authentic) extracts from reference books follow, classifying the nature of the sago tree and the harvesting of its crop throughout history. The narrative device is clumsy, the material presented probably essential to the developing story but tedious to read— effectively it is unworthy of the earlier technical narrative brilliance that

O'Brien displayed in *The Third Policeman*. His scope might have been larger than it was in his previous novels written in the sixties, and it is undoubtedly unfair to pass judgment on a work that not only is incomplete but may also have been subject to revisions. Nevertheless, it is highly unlikely that *Sago Saga* would have been O'Brien's new masterpiece. As the manuscript has been published, however, what there is of it needs some kind of comment. Perhaps it is best to remember how ill O'Brien was when he was working on it and to leave the last word on it to him:

I'm still under drug treatment and have to go back at the end of this month for blood transfusions. In other words—never a dull moment but total stasis of that literary project that has come to be called SSS—SLATTERY'S SAGO SAGA. I have finished 73 quarto pages in final typescript, or seven chapters; the scene is set and the characters established ready for the main paroxysms of bedlam, which is planned to take place in the U.S. and culminates in the election of a President. Though never stated, the analogy with the Kennedy reign will not escape the attention of any reader over the age of 8. No censure of the late J.F.K. will be implied but I do consider Old Joe a crook and the two Senator bostoons as lickspittle time-servers, eternally dining out on the late President's corpse.[2]

Slattery's Sago Saga would have been a comic novel like its predecessors; whatever form he turned his mind to, O'Brien was essentially a comic writer. But this notion should not blind us to the fact that the impulse of clowning was always a result of something fundamentally serious or sinister. He might have dismissed *At Swim-Two-Birds* as "juvenile scriviny," but it was a response to writers who had, in his opinion, taken themselves and their art too seriously. O'Brien mocked them by taking their "experiments" to excess. (He disliked the word's use with reference to fiction—it made him think of chemists.) Of the many ways in which *At Swim* can be read, one is as a piece of corrective laughter aimed at the modernists.

The Third Policeman, though hilarious, ultimately has as its subjects isolation and loss of identity, neither of which can be taken lightly. In this novel in particular it is as though O'Brien recognized the abyss beneath the pavement that Virginia Woolf saw, or "the horror, the horror" that Conrad believed was barely kept in place by the veneer of civilization. O'Brien's response, though, was quite different from theirs: he countered despair with comedy, which action is not at all the same as refusing to acknowledge it. In many ways his work is closer to Samuel Beckett's than to the modernist writers of the 1920s. Beckett presents an absurd and meaningless world, managing nevertheless to make us laugh at it.

The Poor Mouth addresses itself to wildly exaggerated rural poverty and sends up the Celtic Twilight/Gaelic League approach that romanticized such things. The book does not jeer at *The Islandman*—which it parodies—because Ó Crohan's book was a sincere and valuable record of his life on the Blasket Islands. O'Brien's later novels, *The Hard Life* and *The Dalkey Archive,* are about urban squalor and the terrifying possibility that things may not always be what they seem. If we stop to consider what we are amused by, we may well be appalled; this point is precisely why O'Brien is worth reading.

His ideas about art were paradoxical, and based not on self-depreciation but on the belief that it is fatal to take oneself too seriously. In some ways his "Myles na gCopaleen" persona is treacherous to enlist in the cause of helping to establish O'Brien's beliefs; reservations have to be made. It would be wrong to say "this is O'Brien's opinion" when it is actually "Myles's"—but it is possible to see what questions interested the writer, because he returned to them in his *Irish Times* column. His response to the Rouault picture (discussed in the first chapter of this book) raises questions concerned with modern art. With the same painting in mind he wrote that the modern artist's success "depends on the customer's taste, education and upbringing. Thus modern art tends to surround itself with 'difficulties.' You must know about it, be told about it, go to lectures in freezing halls."[3] Strikingly, there is no apparent irony at work here. It is true that Myles gently parodies his usual directness by adopting the pose of a lecturer—self-conscious stage directions in parentheses break up the discourse and leaven the pronouncements. Two sentences after expressing a surprising opinion—"But the main thing to bear in mind is the unimportance of all art. It is very much a minority activity"—Myles concludes, "(Suddenly rings bell for morning period; class look at each other, mooch out shifty-eyed)." He retreats into his persona before we can accuse him of being too serious.

Myles—and O'Brien too, if we judge by *At Swim*—holds two views: (a) that art *is* a minority activity and hence "unimportant" and (b) that it is a subject worth returning to in the columns of a daily newspaper. His ability to hold two seemingly opposed opinions is realistic and inevitably paradoxical rather than inconsistent. Audiences, onlookers, and readers must be prepared to educate themselves sufficiently in order to make informed judgments; they must not allow themselves to become self-

indulgent. Myles reserves as much contempt for aesthetes as for those who
reject modern art with naive outrage:

Search any old lukewarm bath and you will find one of these aesthetical
technicians enjoying himself. All round this person in the bath life is going on,
nothing is ever lost. . . . This is life, and stuffed contentedly in the china bath
sits the boy it was invented for, morbidly aware of the structure of history. . . .
[H]e is up to his chin in the carpediurnal present, and simultaneously, in
transcendent sense-immediacy, sensible that without *him,* without *his* feeling, *his*
observation, *his* diapassional apprehension on all planes, *his* non-pensionable
function as a catalyst, the whole filmy edifice would crumble into dust.

Myles seems to anticipate and reject the kind of literary criticism that
panders to critics' egos by placing them in an inordinately superior
position to the work they are considering: "He likes the lukewarm water.
He likes himself liking the lukewarm water. He likes himself liking
himself liking the lukewarm water." The Chinese-box structure of *At
Swim* is brought to mind at this point, because it is designed to provoke,
invite, and parody such self-awareness. Aesthetics, he goes on to say, "is a
mental ailment, the perversion whereby the sufferer believes that to be
consistently . . . *passive* is the prime bacon, the *summum bonham.* The
perfect aesthete logically feels that the artist is strictly a turkish bath
attendant."[4]

These are important statements, and it is typical of and germane to
O'Brien's ideas about art that they should be expressed in terms that
border on the ludicrous—"prime bacon"—and that they should be
presented in a newspaper, which has a currency denied to academic
treatises and, paradoxically, is also ephemeral and therefore inaccessible.
O'Brien wrote without the expectation that many of his articles would be
collected after his death. If one is interested in art, then it is important;
but it must never be treated too solemnly by artists or the public. This
view sums up the attitude underlying the Myles and O'Brien personas. It
is to be found underpinning the writer's fiction and his—equally un-
orthodox—criticism.

In "Cruiskeen Lawn" his targets were pretension of all kinds and
ignorance in those educated enough to know better. Typically, he would
take a particular subject and turn it into a fantasy so elaborate that the
original point would be lost in sheer enjoyment. That is the case with
Myles's *buchhandlung* service. It began as a joke directed at those who do
not read but who are aware that books signify culture: "My friend is a

man of great wealth and vulgarity. . . . Whether he can read or not I do not know, but some savage faculty for observation told him that most respectable and estimable people usually had a lot of books in their houses."[5] The books, Myles notes, are new and remain unopened. Why on earth, he asks himself, should a wealthy person be "put to the trouble of pretending to read at all?" He suggests a "handling" service to imply that the books have been well used. For appropriate fees, different classes of handling are available, from "Popular" to "Handling Superb." Not content to leave the matter there, he introduces refinements, such as forging affectionate messages from authors to owners: "I remain, as ever, your friend and admirer, G. Bernard Shaw"; "from your devoted friend and follower, K. Marx."[6]

The cliché is brought into service too. Book handling leads Myles to the subject of criticism and the unimaginative reviewer's cry "I couldn't put it down." A volume treated with invisible glue would, he suggests, ensure that the hackneyed phrase be used with accuracy for once. Over the years, columns of the *Irish Times* were devoted to Myles na gCopaleen's catechism of cliché. Using clichés himself in describing his intent, he introduced the venture: "A unique compendium of all that is nauseating in contemporary writing. Compiled without regard to expense or feelings of the public. A harrowing survey of sub-literature and all that is pseudo, mal-dicted and calloused in the underworld of print."[7] O'Brien valued precision in writing and detested the inflated style and formula of popular journalism: "Is a man ever hurt in a motor smash? No. He sustains injury. Does such a man ever die from his injuries? No. He succumbs to them. . . . Did he go into the hospital, or enter it, or be brought to it? He did not. He was admitted to it."[8]

So extensive is his treatment of the humble cliché that he quite clearly delighted in the ridiculousness of such overuse. This delight is something he shared with Beckett—clichés are not, after all, confined to journalism. O'Brien and Beckett both make good use of the hackneyed phrase in their fiction because they use it, paradoxically, in a new way. We all use clichés at one time or another. Such phrases are ready-made common property. Because they are universally recognized formulae, they will also function to prevent real contemplation. We can put uncomfortable feelings firmly behind us, safe in a ritual utterance. It is the ability of the stock phrase to prevent thought that makes it so dangerous.

When Beckett uses the phrase "such pleasure that pleasure was not the word,"[9] our attention is arrested. In the work of a more mundane writer, we would not give it a second thought, but because of Beckett's peculiar idiosyncratic use of language, the phrase is defamiliarized. O'Brien too was a master of such usage. In *At Swim* the phrase "a nice cup of tea" becomes extraordinary when it is used in conjunction with the word *paralysis*. "Paralysis is a nice cup of tea" makes us stop and consider. It may provoke a smile, but if it is examined closely it becomes apparent that the phrase is meaningless and arbitrary. Spoken language that is common to us all, placed in the context of a self-conscious literary work, suddenly becomes strange. The cliché in O'Brien's fiction is the reverse of common currency. Instead of being a refuge from thought, it is (to coin a phrase) forged anew; it becomes original and thought-provoking.

O'Brien used puns, too, with something of the verve with which he used clichés. If the latter in common use represent language at its most tired and repetitious, then puns, as is often noted, are the lowest and most tedious form that passes for wit. Undoubtedly, however, O'Brien's audacity and ingenuity have to be admired. Keats and Chapman were his main vehicles, and they appeared in "Cruiskeen Lawn."[10] Half the pleasure in the outrageous awfulness of O'Brien's punning comes from the accumulation of detail leading up to the punch line; however, I will be content here to summarize the first of countless Keats and Chapman episodes. Chapman's pigeon is sick, and he takes it to his friend Keats for help. Keats opens its beak, peers inside, and removes a tiny object obstructing the bird's windpipe. He then sits down and writes a poem, "On First Looking into Chapman's Homer." The reader needs to know that Chapman was a seventeenth-century poet who translated Homer into English, and that the romantic poet John Keats wrote a sonnet entitled "On First Looking into Chapman's Homer" in tribute when he first read Chapman's translation. Comedy evaporates when we dissect and analyze the joke. It is enough to say that O'Brien produced a classic pun by making a phrase serve a totally different function in a different context. This fact in itself should help to explain his predilection: puns are another instance of the instability of language. The same words—or indeed, as an acceptable variation, words that *sound* the same—used in different contexts indicate that the "meaning" of language is not fixed, that language is in fact a system of signs with no intrinsic meaning or reference.

The real Chapman was dead long before Keats was born, but in O'Brien's fantastic imagination the two are contemporaries. In the pages of the *Irish Times* they visit Dublin, Boston, Paris, and places farther afield; they are usually short of money. It is Keats who always delivers the pun.

The usual response to a pun is a groan rather than merry laughter, but O'Brien was not the first writer to use puns extensively. Vivian Mercier points out that Joyce's *Finnegans Wake* "is the apotheosis of the pun."[11] Whereas *Ulysses* was an odyssey that took place over the space of 18 daytime and/or waking hours, *Finnegans Wake* presents nighttime and the unconscious world of dreams. Joyce used puns in *Ulysses*, but they are present in every line of *Wake*. The title itself is an example of double meaning because in Joyce's hands it refers to a funeral party and also incorporates a contradictory sense of the word *wake*, the verb *to wake*. Into the funeral party come suggestions of waking up and implications of rebirth; it is no surprise to find that at one point a funeral becomes a "funferall." With consummate appropriateness Joyce employed puns to create a world of a dreaming mind. In dreams it is not possible to distinguish between fantasy and reality; nothing is tangible and truth is impossible to establish.

Mercier also contends that the pun is the oldest form of wit and wordplay. Acknowledging that verbal play "lies at the root, not merely of Gaelic literature, but of *every* literature,"[12] Mercier claims nevertheless that "the archaic, tradition-bound nature of Gaelic literature and culture preserved into modern times something of the ancient, playful attitude to language, thus creating in English-speaking Ireland a climate favorable to the growth of the great Anglo-Irish wits."[13] This perspective is helpful, for Mercier's scholarly discussion of riddles and puns in early Irish texts and in the later writing of Jonathan Swift, Thomas Sheridan, and John Philpot Curran[14] allows us to place O'Brien in a long cultural tradition— not after Joyce, but in which Joyce also appears.

O'Brien's use of puns was not confined to the columns of "Cruiskeen Lawn" any more than his use of clichés was. The most memorable comes toward the end of *At Swim-Two-Birds,* when Teresa, the servant girl, has saved Trellis's life by burning Orlick's manuscript. Trellis views her rear thoughtfully: "the edge of her stays, lifting her skirt in a little ridge behind her, dipped softly from side to side with the rise and fall of her haunches as she trod the stairs. It is the function of such garments to improve the figure, to conserve corporal discursiveness, to create the illusion of a finely modulated body. If it betrays its own presence when fulfilling this task, its purpose must largely fail. 'Ars est celare artem,' muttered Trellis, doubtful as to whether he had made a pun" (216). To be pedantic, one well-known form of punning rests on words from different languages that sound the same but have entirely different meanings. The gap in this case is between the Latin *ars,* meaning "art," and the English word *arse,* which in Britain is interchangeable with *backside* or *bum.* But the beauty of this particular pun is that it reflects not only on Teresa's corsets, which fail to produce the desired effect, but also on the whole novel. If one accepts the dictum "true art is to conceal art," then *At Swim* fails, for quite deliberately O'Brien makes sure that all of the mechanics of writing fiction are exposed in *At Swim.*

Clichés and puns are comparatively humble devices that we may not immediately think of as being "literary." The same could be said of anecdotes, which also feature largely in O'Brien's writing, often in a surprisingly sophisticated way. The strategy usually takes the form of repeating a story someone told the writer; the technique seems straight-forward enough, but it mirrors O'Brien's whole attitude to writing. The private individual, the author, should be at least one remove from his material. Another way of saying this is to recognize that Flann O'Brien and Myles na gCopaleen were not one and the same as Brian O'Nolan. The first-person narratives of the novels multiply the levels of removal; the adopted persona of the author adopts yet another persona—Bonaparte, Finbarr, the student writing *At Swim,* and the dead narrator of *The Third Policeman.* In such fundamental ways O'Brien produced illusions of distance between himself and his writing. To find the same device in "A Bash in the Tunnel," the critical essay he wrote on James Joyce, is, then, less surprising than it may at first seem.[15]

The title itself is quixotic and unhelpful, explained only by the bizarre anecdote O'Brien first relates, then uses as a metaphor for the position of the artist in Ireland. O'Brien tells us he was quietly drinking in the Scotch House in Dublin when he was approached by a stranger. Over the inevitable drinks, the stranger tells a long, involved story about illegal drinking in the lavatory of a dining carriage in a railway train, left in a siding. This vision becomes an image of the artist's position in Ireland. As far as O'Brien's drinking companion is concerned, a "bash in the cars" is a very good thing to have. But the "bash in the tunnel" that occurred inadvertently was another thing. The stranger says, "I always try to see, for the good of me health, that a bash doesn't last more than a day and a night." He does not wear a watch but knows that it is night when it is dark outside, day if it is bright. And so when he was shunted into a tunnel and left there, his system broke down: "Here was meself parked in the tunnel opening bottle after bottle in the dark, thinking the night was a very long one" (205). "Funny?" O'Brien comments. "But surely there you have the Irish artist? Sitting fully dressed, innerly locked in the toilet of a locked coach where he had no right to be, resentfully drinking somebody else's whiskey, being whisked hither and thither by anonymous shunters, keeping fastidiously the while on the outer face of his door the simple word, ENGAGED" (206). Anecdotal, but not easy to understand the application in spite of that. In O'Brien's opinion the image fits Joyce.

This account is followed not by elucidation but by another anecdote, in this instance involving a friend of O'Brien's, a man who, at a dinner, found himself sitting next to someone whom Joyce had fictionalized in *Ulysses*. The "character" and the friend remain nameless; the point of the story is the way in which real people can become "legendary and fictional" if a writer bases a fictional character on them: a preposterous inversion of the popular but misguided belief that, to use O'Brien's example, "there once lived a man named Sherlock Holmes." Niall Sheridan's astonishment at finding himself leading a double life—his real one and a fictional existence as the character Brinsley in *At Swim-Two-Birds*—is akin to the response of the outraged dinner guest, who neglects wine and cigars to angrily assert that he not only was alive but had published books of his own: "How can I be a character in fiction . . . if I am here talking to you?"

It is irrelevant to ask whether these two anecdotes are real or invented. They are told to raise questions and to subvert the nature of more conventional criticism. They deliberately offer no answers—but not because O'Brien was incapable of handing his readers insights, had he wished to do so. The last page of his essay briefly mentions other essays in the special "Joyce" issue of *Envoy* that "A Bash in the Tunnel" introduced, and O'Brien points out that none of the other contributors comment on Joyce's humor. Succinctly he rectifies this omission: "Humour, the handmaid of sorrow and fear, creeps out endlessly in Joyce's works. He uses the thing in the same way as Shakespeare does but less formally, to attenuate the fear of those who have belief and who genuinely think that they will be in hell or in heaven shortly, and possibly very shortly. . . . True humour needs this background urgency: Rabelais is funny but his stuff cloys. His stuff lacks tragedy" (208). It is unsurprising that O'Brien should identify this particular quality which he himself shares with Joyce. Comedy is addressed in all seriousness; criticism is not. He sums up the fascination Joyce exerts over his readers—secretiveness, ambiguity, leg-pulling, dishonesties, technical skill: "His works are a garden in which some of us may play. This issue of *Envoy* claims to be merely a small bit of that garden." From however many perspectives Joyce is viewed, there is no possibility of providing a

key or an exhaustive interpretation of his work, for "at the end Joyce will
still be in his tunnel, unabashed." The final pun, referring to O'Brien's
own anecdotal starting point, reveals characteristic attitudes: (a) dif-
fidence—a refusal to offer readers of the Joyce special issue an easy (and
thus untruthful) "answer" to the difficulties Joyce presents; and (b)
ambivalence in O'Brien's own attitude—he does not address his subject
directly but sees Joyce as someone doubly locked in darkness, conscious
only of himself. Yet in O'Brien's use of the word *unabashed* he suggests
that Joyce is aware of his isolation and remains there from choice, forever
beyond explication and exegesis. The essay is a curious backhanded
tribute, revealing as much about O'Brien's perceptions and reticences as it
does about his subject.

O'Brien's diverse work in different fields is not homogenous, but it is
certainly possible to see similar preoccupations emerge. His short stories
are no exception. The substance of "The Martyr's Crown"[16] is an
anecdote one man tells another about a third, younger man they pass in
the street. "John Duffy's Brother"[17] is anecdotal too, but in a more subtle
way that links it with the two earliest novels. It begins with a paradox:
"Strictly speaking this story should not be written or told at all. To write
it or to tell it is to spoil it. This is because the man who had the strange
experience we are going to talk about never mentioned it to anybody, and
the fact that he kept his secret and sealed it up completely in his memory
is the whole point of the story." It is not a first-person narrative, but, like
that of *The Third Policeman,* the position from which it is told is an
untenable one. If the story was never told in the first place, how does the
present narrator know about it—unless it happened to him, and we are,
in fact, reading a disguised first-person narration? The straightforward
answer is that it is O'Brien's invention; nevertheless, the question is valid
because of the gesture toward anecdote: "the man who had the strange
experience *we are going to talk about*" (my emphasis) and the sense of
authenticity this statement aims to confer. It presupposes the attitude
that actual lived experience is fundamental to fiction, a view to which
O'Brien certainly did not subscribe. An unwritten rule of fiction—that
the reader must be allowed the indulgence of believing in the events he
reads about—coexists in the case of "John Duffy's Brother" with a direct
acknowledgment that it is an impossibility: "We must admit that
handicap at the beginning—that it is absurd for us to tell the story,
absurd for anybody to listen to it, and unthinkable that anybody should
believe it" (91). Two contradictory attitudes are presented simultaneously.

The protagonist is, to all intents and purposes, as nameless as the protagonists of *At Swim* and *The Third Policeman*. He is "John Duffy's Brother." The narrator will not identify him further: "there are thousands of these Duffys in the world," and so his anonymity is safeguarded; "this will enable us to tell his secret and permit him to continue looking his friends in the eye." Having admitted the impossibility of the fiction, the storyteller goes to lengths to conceal identity—suggesting a biographical basis: "We do not break faith . . . because even if there are only one hundred John Duffy's in existence, and even if each one of them could be met and questioned, no embarrassing enlightenments would be forthcoming. That is because the John Duffy in question never left his house, never left his bed, never talked to anybody in his life and was never seen by more than one man. That man's name was Gumly. Gumly was a doctor. He was present when John Duffy was born and also when he died, one hour later" (92). The elaboration is quite irrelevant to the story that follows, and yet fundamental to the problems and pleasures of narrative fiction—which are the real subject of the story.

The diction of "John Duffy's Brother" is similar to that of the early novels. The river Liffey is like a "respectable married man," the point of the bizarre comparison being that "it seemed to be hurrying into Dublin as if to work." Each morning the inhabitants of Chapelizod "would erect, as if for Mr. Duffy's benefit, a lazy plume of smoke to show exactly where they were." And the direct comment on the fiction—"modern writing, it is hoped, has passed the stage when simple events are stated in the void"—has something of *At Swim's* self-reflexiveness.

John Duffy's brother has a kind of brainstorm on the way to work one morning and believes he is a train. He is humored by his fellow office workers, who assume he is perpetrating an elaborate joke. This continues throughout the morning. He gets up steam at 12:45 P.M. so that he can depart promptly at 1:00, lets out a shrill whistle, and steams out of the office. In the middle of lunch, however, "John Duffy's brother felt something important, something queer, momentous and magical taking place inside his brain" (96). No longer a train, he is a "badly frightened man." Though something terrifying has occurred, he passes the mental aberration off lightly when he returns to work, saying, "I'm afraid the train is a bit late getting back." His colleagues' weak smiles assure him that "a morning's joke was not good enough for the same evening," and he is thus certain that his secret madness is safe. We are told that the "strange malady" never returned, but the insight Duffy gained into the workings of his mind remains to haunt him: "[T]o this day [he] starts at the rumble of a train in the Liffy tunnel and stands rooted to the road when he comes suddenly on a level crossing—silent, so to speak, upon a peak in Darien" (97).

The final pun, if it can be so called in this context, comes from Keats's sonnet "On First Looking into Chapman's Homer." But it serves a very different purpose here from the amusing use to which O'Brien put it in "Cruiskeen Lawn." Keats uses Cortés's discovery of a newfound land as an analogy for his own sense of wonder at discovering Chapman's translation of Homer:

> Then felt I like some watcher of the skies
> When a new planet swims into his ken;
> Or like stout Cortez when with eagle eyes
> He stared at the Pacific—and all his men
> Looked at each other with a wild surmise—
> Silent upon a peak in Darien.[18]

New, exhilarating, terrifying, and strange—new horizons are opened for the explorer, for the poet Keats, and for John Duffy's brother, the inoffensive, quiet citizen of Inchicore who would have preferred the unfathomable depths of his mind to have remained undiscovered.

Such lengthy comment may seem disproportionate to the slightness of "John Duffy's Brother," but though the story *can* be read and dismissed as simply amusing, it is a not-inconsiderable achievement. The moment of self-awareness, "the really important part of the plot, the incident which gives the whole story its significance" (96), belongs to the brother of John Duffy; but the narrative comments on the absurdity of telling a tale that is spoiled if it is written or told at all refer the moment of insight to all readers of fiction. It emphasizes the subtleties and paradox of the narrator's untenable position, and it sends up the sophisticated reader who is pedantic enough to work out the technical sleight of hand. Like *At Swim-Two-Birds,* the story is, as O'Brien said of Joyce's work, "a garden in which some of us may play." The best of O'Brien's fiction all have this ludic—or playful—quality. The main pleasures of the game are the inexhaustible possibilities of narrative that are alternately exposed and hidden.

Chapter Eight

Flann O'Brien and Other Novelists

Trying to establish the influence of one writer on another is usually an unprofitable occupation, but in O'Brien's case there is no doubt that he exerted and continues to exert an imaginative hold over other novelists who have paid tribute to him in their own fiction. Gilbert Sorrentino takes an epigraph for his novel *Mulligan Stew* from O'Brien's *Third Policeman;* Alasdair Gray adds a deliberately facetious footnote to *Lanark* citing O'Brien; B. S. Johnson's *Travelling People* opens with a preface that reads like eighteenth-century prose but is also a pastiche of the opening of *At Swim.*

It is true to say that all these writers—and John Fowles should be included in their number—have, as did O'Brien, an interest in what has come to be called self-reflexive fiction, or metafiction, which was certainly not invented by O'Brien. Briefly, self-reflexive fiction usually takes as its main subject fiction itself. The impulse runs counter to, but is dependent on, more mainstream realist novels that aim to convey to readers that they are telling true stories and that we are reading about the same world we inhabit; there are no problems about translating actions or feelings into prose. By contrast, self-reflexive fiction exposes literary devices, things we might not even be aware of when reading more conventional novels, such as the selection of events that are recounted, and the style in which they are told. By drawing such devices to the reader's attention and making them part of the text itself, the metanovelists achieve a different kind of "honesty": life is not necessarily neat and tidy, and fiction is incapable of incorporating every detail.

Laurence Sterne used the device as long ago as the eighteenth century in *The Life and Opinions of Tristram Shandy.* Tristram continually tells his reader how harassed he is by the inevitable fact that his life is lived much more quickly than he can record it. He finds it impossible to tell a straightforward story because of his desire to be comprehensive, and so he is continually obliged to "digress"—to include seemingly irrelevant explanations and anecdotes relating to his family and their obsessions in order to make his readers fully understand why he, Tristram, is as he is. The resultant apparent chaos is actually an illusion; the work is carefully controlled and structured. The digressions, as Tristram himself says, are actually the means of progression, but that is not necessarily our initial experience of the work, any more than it would be were we reading Joyce's *Ulysses* for the first time.

Intractable material is something the narrator of *At Swim* has to deal with, and his method is simply to transcribe into his fiction written documents of any kind that happen to interest him, emphasizing the fact that he is doing so. He includes the fiction that he writes as well as autobiography, but his characters are no more tractable than Sterne's. Like Tristram, he claims to lose large chunks of his manuscript. Effectively he suffers all the problems any writer encounters; the difference is that he incorporates the difficulties. Both books address the problems of writing novels.

There is a difference, then, between setting O'Brien in a particular context of antinovelists and identifying later writers who may fit in that context too but who acknowledge a particular debt to, or delight in, O'Brien's work. B. S. Johnson is one of the few avant-garde novelists I intend to discuss who does not mention O'Brien by name but who seems to have absorbed, however unconsciously, a number of O'Brien's characteristics. His novel, or antinovel, *Travelling People*[1] opens with a statement of intent that follows the opening of *At Swim* and the narrator's aesthetic (25) very closely indeed: "Seated comfortably in a wood and wickerwork chair of eighteenth-century Chinese manufacture, I began seriously to meditate upon the form of my allegedly full-time literary sublimations." It is not one beginning and one ending that he objects to, but his objections are couched in very similar terms to those of O'Brien's narrator: "I decided that one style for a novel was a convention that I resented most strongly." By implication Joyce had come to the same conclusion, and expressed it in the multiple styles of *Ulysses*. And so, unlikely though it may seem, Johnson was writing in an established tradition. But at the same time, his diction and the cadences of his sentences echo those of O'Brien:

I should be determined not to lead my reader into believing that he was doing anything but reading a novel, having noted with abhorrence the shabby chicanery practised on their readers by many novelists, particularly of the popular class. This applied especially to digression, where the reader is led, wilfully and wantonly, astray; my novels would have clear notice, one way or another, of digressions, so that the reader might have complete freedom of choice in whether or not he would read them.

Thus, having decided in a general way upon the construction of my novel, I thought about actually rising to commence its composition; but persuaded by oriental comfort that I was nearer the Good Life engaged in meditation, I turned my mind to the deep consideration of such other matters as I deemed worthy of my attention, and, after a short while thus engaged, fell asleep.[2]

Attitudes and persona, as well as style, recall O'Brien's narrator. Yet the experience of reading *Travelling People* is very different from that of reading *At Swim*. Johnson's novel is essentially linear and chronological; it focuses on Henry, his protagonist, a focus that ensures the book never becomes as anarchic or bewildering as *At Swim-Two-Birds*. Commenting on the explanatory "Prelude" to *Travelling People,* part of which is quoted in the foregoing excerpt, Johnson says that it was "deliberately a pastiche of eighteenth-century English, for I had found that it was necessary to return to the very beginnings of the novel in England in order to re-think it and rejustify it for myself."[3] He says that the most obvious of his debts was to *Tristram Shandy,* and fails to mention O'Brien at all, but this omission is fair enough, particularly as O'Brien himself was deliberately misleading and inconsistent about attributing sources and influences. Spotting them becomes part of the game such texts offer.

Like O'Brien and Beckett before him, Johnson also ironically describes his protagonist by means of a table. He lists 18 points, including age, weight, height, and chest and waist measurements. Readers would not expect to find information presented this way in realistic novels; like O'Brien and Beckett, Johnson affirms his affiliations with the countertradition, impatient with the too-easy assumption that truth can be conveyed at all.

Most novelists who refer to O'Brien take their allusions from either *At Swim* or *The Third Policeman;* that they do so is in itself an indication of the consensus regarding these books' stature compared with that of O'Brien's later fiction. It is interesting, then, to recognize undergraduate humor emerging in *Travelling People*—appropriate to the recently graduated Henry—that is similar to one of O'Brien's flights of fancy in "Cruiskeen Lawn." Henry Henry—his given name and surname are the same—imagines setting up a service for the public: "Henry Henry Conversation arranged with the Nobility on their Own Terms. Conversation suffered with the Wealthy on his Own Terms. Do not be taken in by

Spurious Imitators. Henry Conversation has that Inner Glow. Have
Henry Henry for your Hunt Balls."[4] Writing as "Myles," O'Brien
invented the "Myles na gCopaleen Escort Service," a team of ventrilo-
quists, each one of whom "answers his own manly questions in a voice far
pleasanter than your unfeminine quack, and gives answers that will
astonish the people behind for their brilliance and sparkle."[5]

If B. S. Johnson fails to mention O'Brien by name, Alasdair Gray goes
to the opposite extreme and provides footnotes in the epilogue to *Lanark,*
citing O'Brien, among countless other writers, in a fine display of
erudition. The footnote is intentionally irrelevant; it provides an incisive
comic criticism of Gray's own fiction, and, of course, it is written by Gray
himself. In *At Swim* Brinsley is allowed to criticize the narrator's
manuscript, and he is usually dismissive of his friend's work. Objections
raised within the text are relatively common in self-reflexive fiction.

In his footnote, Gray identifies a source for *At Swim* that O'Brien
certainly never admitted and that to my knowledge has not been noted by
any other commentator:

The hero's biography after death occurs in Wyndham Lewis's trilogy *The Human
Age,* Flann O'Brien's *The Third Policeman* and Golding's *Pincher Martin.* . . .
Monboddo's speech in the last part of *Lanark* is a dreary parody of the Archangel
Michael's history lecture in the last book of *Paradise Lost* and fails for the same
reason. A property is not always valuable because it is stolen from a rich man.
And for this single device thieved (without acknowledgment) from Milton we
find a confrontation of fictional character by fictional author from Flann O'Brien;
a hero ignorant of his past, in a subfuse modern Hell, also from Flann O'Brien;
and from T. S. Eliot, Nabokov and Flann O'Brien, a parade of irrelevant
erudition through grotesquely inflated footnotes.[6]

Of which Gray's are a perfect example. In case we miss it, O'Brien's name
is cross-referenced in a list of writers Gray claims to have plagiarized, the
list printed as a parallel text to the epilogue. Both Gray and B. S. Johnson
use print on the page in unusual ways. Like the black page that indicates
mourning for Parson Yorick in *Tristram Shandy,* pages of varying degrees
of grayness appear in *Travelling People* to indicate the progress of a heart
attack and the subsequent death of one of Johnson's characters. In the
interests of approximating "real life" as precisely as possible, O'Brien in
At Swim prints diagrams of gas meters to explain how to read them. The
book as a technological object is exploited to the fullest.

Gray's footnoting in *Lanark* owes something to *The Third Policeman's*
extravagant use of footnotes that cite de Selby on a number of spurious

issues. But Gray has said that his novel *1982 Janine* owes most to O'Brien: "I partly acknowledge this in the Epilogue, but insufficiently."[7] Gray's epilogue in *Janine* is addressed to the "discerning critic," and after he has listed some 30 writers he is indebted to, he adds that the "narrator without self-respect" is from Dostoyevski, Celine, and "the first-person novels of Flann O'Brien and from Camus's *The Fall*. An elaborate fantasy within a plausible everyday fiction is from Flann O'Brien's *At Swim-Two-Birds*, Nabokov's *Pale Fire*, Vonnegut's *Slaughterhouse Five*."[8]

In a letter to me,[9] Gray raises the question of class and emphasizes the social impartiality of O'Brien's protagonists, a quality he finds appealing, one that his own protagonists share and that he has identified in Irish, French, American, and Russian fiction "but hardly any English." This element of impartiality, he says, is his greatest inheritance from O'Brien.

Intractable characters who refuse to do as their authors wish express the very real frustration novelists must feel when perceiving the gap between the conception of an idea (for example, where the plot will lead) and the execution (which may be quite different). The notion of autonomous characters who seem to be in charge of their own destinies in spite of the writer's wishes is taken quite literally by O'Brien in *At Swim*, whose novelist within the novel, Trellis, is drugged by his characters so that they can continue to lead the lives they wish instead of adopting the roles Trellis tries to impose on them. The narrator who invents Trellis makes his views clear: "It was undemocratic to compel characters to be uniformly good or bad or poor or rich. Each should be allowed a private life, self-determination and a decent standard of living. This would make for self-respect, contentment and better service" (25). At one point in Anthony Burgess's *Earthly Powers* the novelist within that novel, Toomey, goes to his study, sighs, numbers a new sheet of paper, and "recalled some of my characters from their brief sleep and set them talking. They started talking, to my surprise, about the novel that contained them, rather like one of those cartoon films in which anthropomorphic animals get out of their frame and start abusing their creator."[10] Toomey's experience is like that of numerous novelists within novels, but what follows immediately afterward suggests that though countless writers may have had similar thoughts, few have expressed them as succinctly as O'Brien did in *At Swim*. Diana Cartwright, one of Toomey's characters, says, "A novelist friend of mine . . . affirmed that a satisfactory novel should be a self-evident sham to which the reader could regulate at will the degree of his credulity."[11] Toomey's creation must be a friend of O'Brien's narrator, then, for the words are identical to his.

O'Brien's influence within the genre is far-reaching. John Fowles's *Mantissa* can be read as a metaphor for the creative imagination. Miles Green, Fowles's novelist within the novel, engages in numerous power struggles with his female characters—who are ultimately the same character in different manifestations. It is difficult to trust one's judgment as to the specific influence of O'Brien when one reads passages like this one, in which Miles Green addresses his creation Erato: "You've ruined my work from the start. . . . I hadn't the least desire to be what I am when I began. I was going to follow in Joyce and Beckett's footsteps. But oh no, in you trot. . . . Again and again you've made me cut out the best stuff. The text where I had twelve different endings—it was perfect as it was, no one had ever done that before. Then you get at it, and I'm left with just three."[12] Erato is quite capable of standing up to her creator: "When it comes to literary things that need true maturity and experience, like endings, I make decisions. Is that clear?"[13] Momentarily at her mercy, Green submits.

It is only in the last paragraph of the novel that one's sense that O'Brien must be at least partly behind *Mantissa* is confirmed. The author lies not in his stuffy bedroom, as *At Swim's* narrator does, but in a hospital bed. The silence is disrupted only by a cuckoo clock that "cuckoos" as if "obliged one last time to re-affirm its extraneity, its distance from all that has happened in that room, and its undying regard for its first and aesthoautogamous (*Keep the fun clean, said Shanahan*) owner; or as if dream-babbling of green Irish fields and mountain meadows."[14] If Burgess's Diana Cartwright is a friend of *At Swim's* narrator, in the same way one of O'Brian's characters, Shanahan, is keeping an eye on Fowles's text. It is the use of the word *aesthoautogamous* that signals this intrusion and confirms Fowles's approval of O'Brien. "Aestho-auto-gamy," as "Our Medical Correspondent" explains in *At Swim*, "is a very familiar phenomenon in literature" (40). It involves the creation of character while eliminating entirely the procedures of conception and pregnancy. As usual, O'Brien takes the fantasy to its ultimate, seemingly logical conclusion, deliberately blurring the boundaries of art and life by envisaging the day when "the breeding and safe deliverance of Old age Pensioners and other aged and infirm eligible for public money would transform matrimony from the sordid struggle that it often is to an advantageous business enterprise of limitless possibilities" (41). Between them, first O'Brien and then Fowles have invented their own erotics of narrative.

Miles Green asserts that serious modern fiction "has only one subject:

the difficulty of writing serious modern fiction. First, it has fully accepted that it is only fiction, can only be fiction, will never be anything but fiction, and therefore has no business at all tampering with real life or reality"[15]—an efficient summary of the role of the self-reflexive novel in the twentieth century.

Fowles can no longer remember whether naming his character "Miles" had any reference to O'Brien's "Myles" persona.[16] But Gilbert Sorrentino takes "Anthony Lamont," "Shelia," and "Dermot" from *At Swim*, as well as prefacing his book with an epigraph from *The Third Policeman*. He dedicates *Mulligan Stew* "to the memory of Brian O'Nolan—his virtue *hilaritas*,"[17] thus offering a generous and well-deserved tribute.

Each of the novelists I have mentioned has taken the avant-garde into other directions too, or has engaged with issues that O'Brien does not address; nonetheless, each acknowledges his debt to O'Brien, either openly or more subtly. Other novelists have done so too. But this chapter is not intended to be a catalog. The intention is to indicate the regard in which O'Brien is held, not by critics or academics, whom he is likely to have scorned or laughed at, but by creative writers like himself.

Notes and References

Chapter One

1. Letter to Elisabeth Shank, 13 April 1965.
2. Interview by Peter Duval-Smith for the BBC radio program "Bookstand"; from a transcript in the BBC Written Archives Centre.
3. *Guardian*, 19 January 1966.
4. "Cruiskeen Lawn," *Irish Times*, 13 April 1960.
5. Timothy O'Keeffe, ed., *Myles: Portraits of Brian O'Nolan* (London: Martin Brian & O'Keeffe, 1973), 14–15. References to essays in this volume are hereafter cited as "O'Keeffe, ed."
6. Ciaran O'Nolan, *Óige An Dearthár* (*The Brothers' Youth*) (Dublin: 1973), 62. Translation supplied by John Wyse Jackson.
7. Ibid., 63.
8. O'Keeffe, ed., *Myles*, 25.
9. Ibid., 26.
10. Ibid.
11. *Guardian*, 19 January 1966.
12. Anthony Cronin, *Dead as Doornails* (Dublin: Poolbeg Press, 1980), 110.
13. O'Keeffe, ed., *Myles*, 36.
14. *Envoy*, 17 May 1951; reprinted in *Stories and Plays*, ed. Claud Cockburn, (London: Grafton Books, 1986).
15. John Wyse Jackson, ed., *Myles before Myles* (London: Grafton Books, 1988), 50.
16. Ibid., 79.
17. O'Keeffe, ed., *Myles*, 40.
18. Ibid.
19. Ibid., 42.
20. *At Swim-Two-Birds* (Harmondsworth: Penguin, 1967), 12; another letter from the same source appears on p. 37. All quotations from *At Swim* are from this edition.
21. O'Keeffe, ed., *Myles*, 20.
22. "Cruiskeen Lawn," *Irish Times*, 2 March 1966.
23. Kevin O'Nolan, ed., *The Best of Myles* (London: Picador, 1977), 243–44.
24. "Cruiskeen Lawn," *Irish Times*, 13 August 1959.
25. *Myles before Myles*, 17.

26. Ibid., 97.

27. O'Keeffe, ed., *Myles*, 61.

28. Ibid.

29. "Cruiskeen Lawn," *Irish Times*, 4 February 1965.

30. John Ryan, *Remembering How We Stood* (Dublin: Gill & Macmillan, 1975), 20.

31. Ibid., 19.

32. Ibid., 18.

33. Ibid., 19.

34. *The Best of Myles*, 236.

35. Ibid.

36. *Myles before Myles*, 186.

37. Cronin, *Dead as Doornails*, 115.

38. Letter to Brian Inglis, 17 August 1960.

39. Cronin, *Dead as Doornails*, 117.

40. Ibid.

41. Letter, 21 September 1962.

42. Ryan, *Remembering How We Stood*, 138.

43. Ibid., 139.

44. Letter to Hugh Leonard, 30 August 1965.

45. Letter to A. Sheil, 17 April 1963.

46. Letter to Con Levantal, 22 March 1965.

47. Letter to O'Keeffe, 15 October 1965.

48. Letter, 16 January 1962.

49. Letter, 1 March 1963.

50. This and the following quotations are from "Can a Saint Hit Back?" *Guardian*, 19 January 1966.

51. Letter to Mark Hamilton, 28 November 1963.

52. Letter, 22 November 1965.

53. Letter to O'Keeffe, 10 July 1965.

54. Letter to Hugh Leonard, 27 August 1965.

55. Letter to Ian Saintsbury, 6 August 1965.

56. Letter to O'Keeffe, 6 July 1965.

57. Letter to Gunnar Rugheimer, 15 March 1966.

58. Ryan, *Remembering How We Stood*, 143.

Chapter Two

1. Letter from Ethel Mannin to O'Brien, 13 July 1939.

2. 14 July 1939.

3. Richard Ellman, *James Joyce* (London: Oxford University Press, 1959), 716.

4. "Mr. Bennett and Mrs. Brown," in *Collected Essays of Virginia Woolf*, ed. Leonard Woolf, vol. 1 (London: Chatto & Windus, 1966).

5. O'Keeffe, ed., *Myles,* 39.

6. James Joyce, *A Portrait of the Artist as a Young Man* (London: Granada, 1977), 185.

7. Ibid., 192.

8. 25 November 1961.

9. O'Keeffe, ed., *Myles,* 49.

10. Page numbers in the text refer to *At Swim-Two-Birds.*

11. *The Aldine Edition of the British Poets,* vol. 12, 1831.

12. O'Keeffe, ed., *Myles,* 44.

13. Ibid., 47.

14. Anne Clissmann, *Flann O'Brien,* (Dublin: Gill & Macmillan, 1975).

15. *Bleak House* (London: Chapman and Hall, 1892).

16. True to the text of the book, the letter adds, "Tactics and Ballistics a Speciality"; the letter is not dated.

17. Robert Adams, *Afterjoyce* (London: Oxford University Press, 1977), 188.

18. Samuel Beckett, *Murphy* (London: Picador, 1977), 10.

19. Vivian Mercier, *The Irish Comic Tradition* (London: Oxford University Press, 1962), 12.

20. Ibid.

21. O'Keeffe, ed., *Myles,* 58.

22. 19 October 1938.

23. Letter from Patience Ross, to A. M. Health, 24 October 1938.

24. O'Keeffe, ed. 38.

25. 15 September 1938.

26. 10 February 1965.

27. Morisset's translation of the title to *Kermesse Irlandaise* provoked O'Brien to comment, "Beat that for side-stepping" (letter to O'Keeffe, 18 March 1965). *Kermesse,* meaning a saturnalian celebration, can be variously translated as *church fete, bazaar,* or even *bedlam;* the word evokes associations of the Roman Catholic Church, and though these associations are not automatically applicable to the word's use, they are probably implied in Morisset's title. The difficulty of finding a precise English translation may have prompted O'Brien's plan for an English-French-English edition of his novel.

28. 12 April 1965.

29. 2 March 1966.

30. 21 April 1965.

31. Laurence Sterne, *The Life and Opinions of Tristram Shandy* (Harmondsworth: Penguin, 1978), 1759–67.

Chapter Three

1. *The Third Policeman* (London: Picador, 1974); all page numbers in the text refer to this edition.

2. 1 May 1939.

3. 14 February 1940.

4. Jonathon Culler, *A Structuralist Poetics* (London: Routledge & Kegan Paul, 1975), 192.

5. Hugh Kenner, *A Colder Eye* (Harmondsworth: Penguin, 1984), 101.

6. 7 September 1940.

7. 14 February 1940.

Chapter Four

1. Page numbers in the text refer to Patrick Power's translation, *The Poor Mouth* (London: Picador, 1976).

2. *The Poor Mouth,* from Patrick Power's "Translator's Preface."

3. Kevin O'Nolan, ed., *The Hair of the Dogma* (London: Hart Davis, 1977), 18.

4. "Cruiskeen Lawn," *Irish Times,* 24 February 1942.

5. Ibid.

6. John Jordan, ed., *The Pleasures of Gaelic Literature* (Cork: Mercier Press, 1977), 28.

7. Peter O'Leary, *My Story* (Cork: Mercier Press, 1970), from the introduction by Cyril T. O'Ceiran, 17.

8. Robin Flower's translation of *The Islandman* (London: Chatto & Windus, 1934), 53.

9. *The Best of Myles,* 276.

10. *The Hair of the Dogma,* 180.

11. O Crohan, *The Islandman,* 297.

12. O'Leary, *My Story,* 44.

13. O Crohan, *The Islandman,* 323.

14. Ibid., 2.

15. Ibid.

16. Ibid., 196.

17. Ibid.

18. Ibid., 288.

19. "Ruairi Beag," in *An Glor,* 17 January 1942; quoted in *Irish University Review* 3, no. 2 (Autumn 1973):136.

20. Brendan Kelly, *"An Béal Bocht,"* in *The Pleasures of Gaelic Literature,* ed. John Jordan (Cork: Mercier Press), 95.

21. Letter to Sean O'Casey, 13 April 1942.

Chapter Five

1. All page numbers in the text refer to *The Hard Life* (London: Picador 1976).

2. 6 November 1961.

3. Letter to A. M. Heath, 20 February 1961.

4. 20 February 1960.
5. Samuel Beckett, *Waiting for Godot* (London: Faber & Faber, 1971), 94.
6. Beckett, *Murphy*.
7. Ibid., 151.
8. Ibid., 154.
9. Letter to Mark Hamilton, 20 February 1961.
10. 6 November 1961.
11. Ibid.
12. 10 August 1961.
13. *Spectator,* 17 November 1961.

Chapter Six

1. Page numbers in the text refer to *The Dalkey Archive* (London: Picador, 1976).
2. 21 September 1962.
3. Letter to O'Keeffe, 1 March 1963.
4. J. W. Dunne, *An Experiment with Time* (London: Macmillan, 1981), 145.
5. Ibid., 15.
6. Ibid., 16.
7. 14 November 1964.
8. Dunne, *Experiment with Time,* 7.
9. 11 December 1963.
10. 21 April 1964.
11. 21 September 1962.
12. 6 January 1964.
13. Ibid.
14. 11 December 1963.
15. 6 January 1964.
16. Interview broadcast by the BBC on 7 March 1962.

Chapter Seven

1. *Slattery's Sago Saga* has been published in *Stories and Plays,* ed. Claud Cockburn (London: Grafton Books, 1986); page numbers in the text refer to this edition.
2. Letter to Cecil Scott, 22 November 1965.
3. *The Best of Myles,* 258.
4. Ibid., 249.
5. Ibid., 17.
6. Ibid., 21.
7. Ibid., 202.
8. Ibid.
9. Beckett, *Murphy,* 6.

10. Selected "Keats and Chapman" stories have been edited by Benedict Kiely in *The Various Lives of Keats and Chapman and the Brother* (London: Grafton Books, 1988).

11. Mercier, *The Irish Comic Tradition*, 80.

12. Ibid., 79.

13. Ibid., 80.

14. Ibid., 95–102.

15. "A Bash in the Tunnel" has been published in *Stories and Plays*.

16. "The Martyr's Crown" has been published in *Stories and Plays*.

17. "John Duffy's Brother" has been published in *Stories and Plays*.

18. John Keats, *The Complete Poems* (Harmondsworth: Penguin, 1976), 72.

Chapter Eight

1. B. S. Johnson, *Travelling People* (London: Constable, 1983).

2. Ibid., 12.

3. B. S. Johnson, "Introduction to *Aren't You Rather Young to Be Writing Your Memoirs?*" in *The Novel Today,* ed. Malcolm Bradbury (London: Fontana, 1977), 160.

4. Johnson, *Travelling People,* 27.

5. *The Best of Myles,* 25.

6. Alasdair Gray, *Lanark* (London: Granada, 1982), 490.

7. Letter from Alasdair Gray to me, July 1989.

8. Alasdair Gray, *1982 Janine* (Harmondsworth: Penguin, 1985).

9. Letter to me, July 1989.

10. Anthony Burgess, *Earthly Powers* (London: Hutchinson, 1980), 520.

11. Ibid., 520.

12. John Fowles, *Mantissa* (London: Granada, 1984), 125.

13. Ibid., 137.

14. Ibid., 190.

15. Ibid., 117.

16. Letter to me, 19 July 1989.

17. Gilbert Sorrentino, *Mulligan Stew* (London: Marion Boyars, 1980).

Selected Bibiliography

PRIMARY WORKS

Novels

At Swim-Two-Birds. 1939. Harmondsworth: Penguin, 1967.
The Dalkey Archive. 1964. London: Picador, 1976.
The Hard Life. 1961. London: Picador, 1976.
The Poor Mouth. (An Béal Bocht, 1941.) London: Picador, 1975.
The Third Policeman. 1967. London: Picador, 1974.

Collected Writings

The Best of Myles. Edited by Kevin O'Nolan. London: Picador, 1977.
Further Cuttings from Cruiskeen Lawn. London: Grafton Books, 1988.
Myles Away from Dublin. Edited by Martin Green. London: Grafton Books 1985.
Myles before Myles. Edited by John Wyse Jackson. London: Grafton Books, 1988.
Stories and Plays. Edited by Claud Cockburn. London: Grafton Books, 1986.
The Various Lives of Keats and Chapman and The Brother. Edited by Benedict Kiley. London: Grafton Books, 1988.

SECONDARY WORKS

Clissmann, Anne. *Flann O'Brien: A Critical Introduction to His Writings.* Dublin: Gill & Macmillan, 1973. Essential reading; the first comprehensive study of O'Brien's life and work.
Costello, Peter, and Peter Van de Kamp. *Flann O'Brien: An Illustrated Biography.* London: Bloomsbury Publishing, 1987. Useful collection of photographs depicting O'Brien, Dublin, its inhabitants, and O'Brien memorabilia.
Cronin, Anthony. *Dead as Doornails.* Dublin: Poolbeg Press, 1980. Cronin's recollections of Flann O'Brien, Brendan Behan, and Patrick Kavanagh.
Imhof, Rudigar. *Alive Alive O.* Dublin: Poolbeg Press; Totowa, N.J.: Barnes

& Noble, 1985. A collection of previously published reviews and journal
articles on O'Brien's writings.

Jump, John. *The Pleasures of Gaelic Literature.* Cork: Mercier Press, 1977.
Includes a chapter on *The Poor Mouth;* other essays in this book provide
useful background information on rural Irish autobiography.

Knight, Stephen. "Forms of Gloom: The Novels of Flann O'Brien." In
Cunning Exiles, edited by D. Anderson and Stephen Knight. Cremorne:
Angus & Robertson, 1974. A survey of O'Brien's novels.

Mercier, Vivien. *The Irish Comic Tradition.* London: Oxford University Press,
1962. Though O'Brien is mentioned only briefly, the book gives useful
background information for placing his comedy in context, as well as for
discerning where it diverges.

Murphy, Gerald. *Ossianic Lore and Romantic Tales of Medieval Ireland.* Cork:
Mercier Press, 1971. Helpful background information for understanding
O'Brien's use of Irish myth.

O'Keeffe, Timothey, ed. *Myles: Portraits of Brian O'Nolan.* London: Martin
Brian & O'Keeffe, 1973. A collection of memoirs by Kevin O'Nolan,
Niall Sheridan, Jack White, and John Garvin. J. C. C. Mayes's essay on
O'Brien's fiction is essential reading.

Ryan, John. *Remembering How We Stood.* Dublin: Gill & Macmillan, 1975.
Recollections of Dublin during the forties and fifties; includes chapters
on O'Brien and other literary figures of the time.

Wain, John. " 'To Write for My Own Race': Notes on the Fiction of Flann
O'Brien." In *A House for the Truth* by John Wain. London: Macmillan,
1972. A survey of O'Brien's fiction.

Index

The Author

Sue Asbee obtained her undergraduate degree at Cambridgeshire College of Arts and Technology; she received an M.A. and a Ph.D. from Queen Mary College, University of London, where she has now taught for a number of years. Her Ph.D. thesis was written on reception theory and Flann O'Brien's *At Swim-Two-Birds*. She specializes in twentieth-century literature, and has published books on Virginia Woolf and T. S. Eliot, as well as articles on Mary Lavin, Margery Allingham, Jeanette Winterson, and others.